Apple Pies & Welsh Cakes

A Family Story

Compiled by Marian Rees

Copyright © 2018 by Marian Rees

Printed in the United Kingdom

First Printing 2018

ISBN 978-0-9542907-2-6

Chalk Ridge Publications

Dedication

This book is dedicated to our four wonderful, kind,
loving, talented children, whose ancestral history
may be glimpsed in the pages that follow.

Foreword

For the past fifteen years, I have been researching our family background and feel that it is now time to put pen to paper, or rather fingers to keyboard, to record some of the information gathered.

Initially, it was many hours in record offices and family history centres that provided the facts. More recently, as increasing numbers of parish records have been transcribed, a great deal has been uncovered online. Perhaps the greatest source of personal information, bringing our forebears to life and giving a little insight into their joys and struggles, has been from family members who have shared the enthusiasm that I have for delving into our history.

Irene Frankland, my Grandfather Leslie's sister, provided some of the older photographs and was perhaps the first to stir my own interest in the family. Sylvia Colman, Leslie's brother Ernest's daughter, also gave me copies of photographs, but her greatest gift was the writing that she sent. Having been raised by her Grandparents Arthur and Ada Frankland (my Great Grandparents) she had so many stories to tell, as recounted by Ada over the course of her growing up. These reminiscences are now recorded here and I hope to do justice to Sylvia's work.

Before delving into the family history, there is someone else I must acknowledge. It is my ever-supportive husband Bill, who has travelled the country with me and helped with the many hours in record offices and graveyards! We have shared some surprising revelations as well as a few blind alleys. The most amazing discovery has been that due to an event in 1803 we are in fact related by more than our own marriage. This was the date of the marriage of my 4x Great Grandfather's brother Robert Pincombe to Elizabeth (Betty) Rowcliffe, Bill's 4x Great Grandfather's sister. So, Bill and I are also distant cousins!

We are now in touch with Elizabeth, formerly Pincombe, **our** fifth cousin, who lives in Canada. Elizabeth is another family history enthusiast and has provided so much of our joint Pincombe/Rowcliffe ancestry information.

I will try to divide the history into separate family groups. Inevitably, there will be overlaps (particularly in this family!) and the whole thing may end in confusion.

Marian

Contents

Key to Families

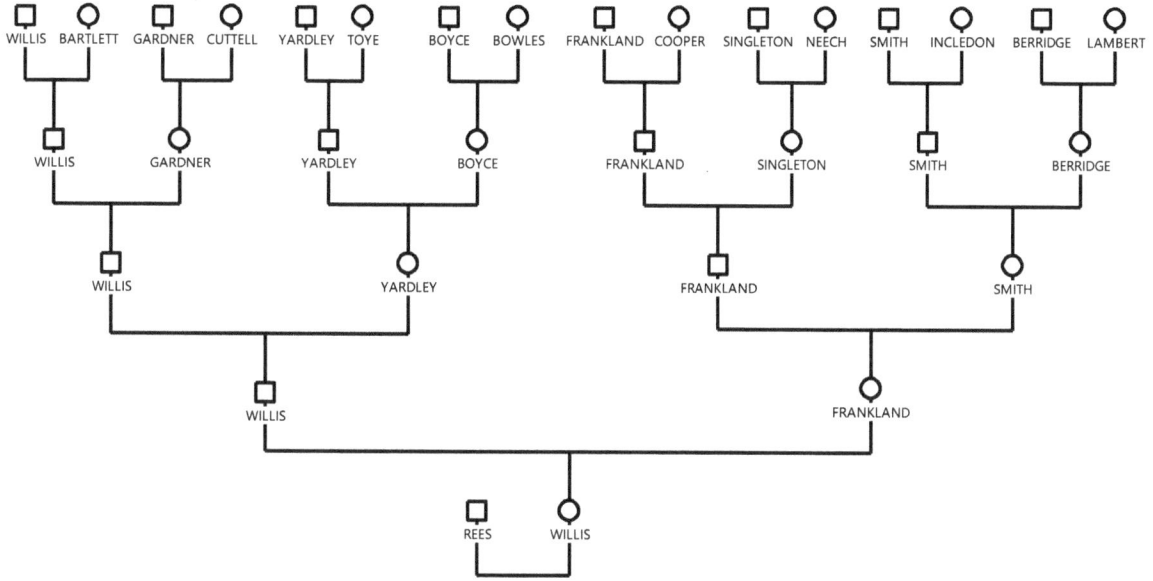

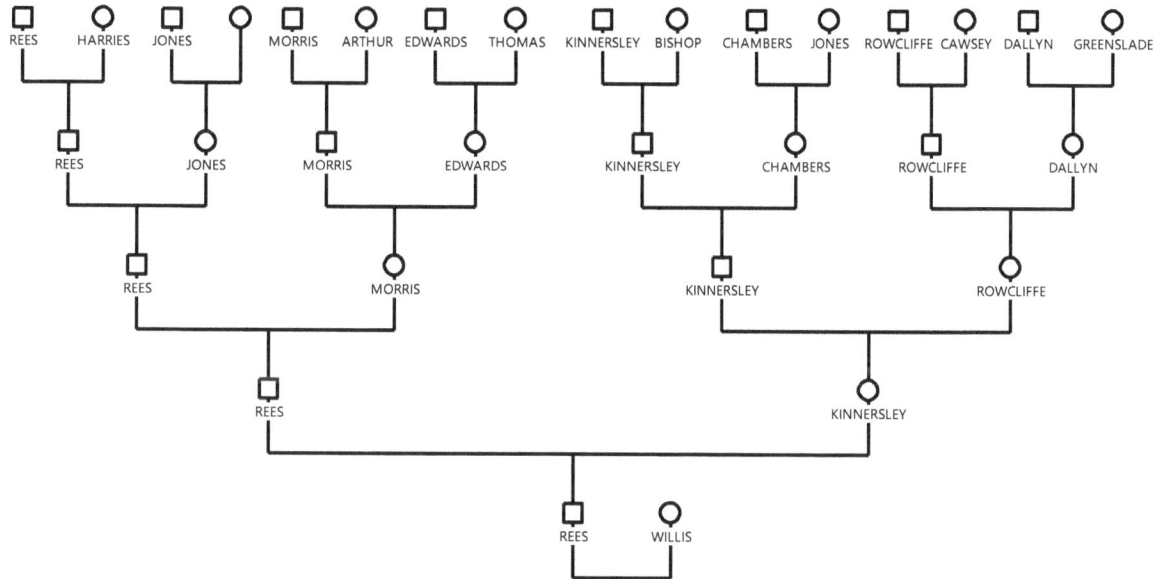

WILLIS · BARTLETT GARDNER · CUTTELL YARDLEY · TOYE BOYCE · BOWLES FRANKLAND · COOPER SINGLETON · NEECH SMITH · INCLEDON BERRIDGE · LAMBERT

WILLIS GARDNER YARDLEY BOYCE FRANKLAND SINGLETON SMITH BERRIDGE

WILLIS YARDLEY FRANKLAND SMITH

WILLIS FRANKLAND

REES · WILLIS

REES · HARRIES JONES MORRIS · ARTHUR EDWARDS · THOMAS KINNERSLEY · BISHOP CHAMBERS · JONES ROWCLIFFE · CAWSEY DALLYN · GREENSLADE

REES JONES MORRIS EDWARDS KINNERSLEY CHAMBERS ROWCLIFFE DALLYN

REES MORRIS KINNERSLEY ROWCLIFFE

REES KINNERSLEY

REES · WILLIS

Historical Timeline

- **1531** Henry VIII head of the newly created Church of England
- **1536** Dissolution of the Monasteries
- **1538** Parish registers kept
- **1588** Spanish Armada destroyed
- **1603** King James VI of Scotland crowned James I of England
- **1605** Gunpowder Plot
- **1620** The Mayflower sailed to the New World
- **1642-1660** Civil War in England
- **1649** Charles I executed - Oliver Cromwell Lord Protector of England
- **1660** Charles II restored as monarch
- **1665-1666** Great Plague followed by Great Fire of London
- **1685** Increase in the migration of Huguenot refugees from France to England.
- **1688-89** William of Orange from Holland crowned King of England
- **1707** England and Wales united with Scotland (United Kingdom)
- **1702** William III succeeded by Anne
- **1714** George I crowned king
- **1752** Gregorian calendar -Year start changed from 25 March to 1 January
- **1754** Lord Hardwicke's Act outlawed marriage outside the Church of England (except for Quakers and Jews)
- **1756-1762** The Seven Years War in North America
- **1756-1765** Industrial revolution began - invention of the steam engine and the spinning jenny.
- **1775-1783** American War of Independence
- **1800** Ireland became part of the United Kingdom
- **1805** Battle of Trafalgar
- **1815** Battle of Waterloo (end of Napoleonic Wars)
- **1830** First railways in England
- **1834** Workhouses were established
- **1837** Civil registration of births, marriages, and deaths began
- **1837-1901** Queen Victoria reigned
- **1841** First genealogically useful census
- **1854-1856** Crimean war
- **1863** First underground train in London
- **1877-1902** Boer Wars
- **1914–1918** World War I
- **1939–1945** World War II.

The Singletons

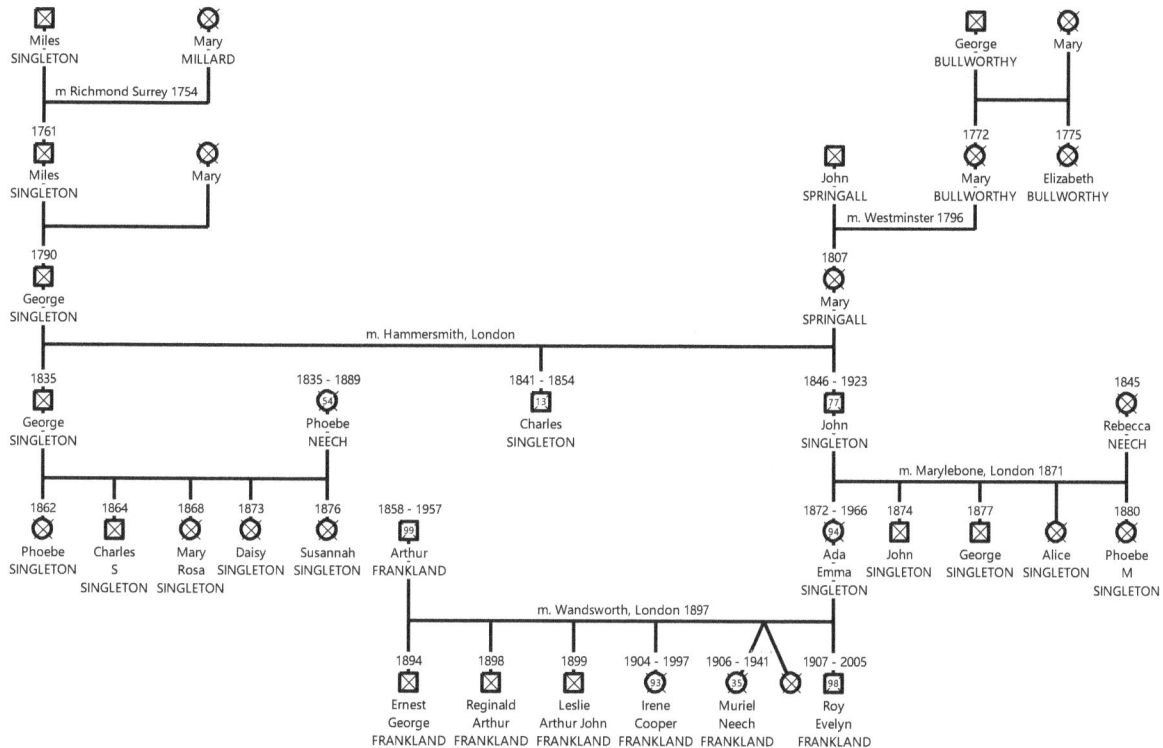

⊠ Miles SINGLETON	⊗ Mary MILLARD			⊠ George BULLWORTHY	⊗ Mary

m Richmond Surrey 1754

1761
⊠ Miles SINGLETON — ⊗ Mary

John SPRINGALL ⊠

1772 Mary BULLWORTHY ⊗ — 1775 Elizabeth BULLWORTHY ⊗

m. Westminster 1796

1790
⊠ George SINGLETON

1807
⊗ Mary SPRINGALL

m. Hammersmith, London

| 1835 ⊠ George SINGLETON | 1835 - 1889 ⊗ 54 Phoebe NEECH | 1841 - 1854 ⊠ 13 Charles SINGLETON | 1846 - 1923 ⊠ 77 John SINGLETON | 1845 ⊗ Rebecca NEECH |

m. Marylebone, London 1871

| 1862 ⊗ Phoebe SINGLETON | 1864 ⊠ Charles S SINGLETON | 1868 ⊗ Mary Rosa SINGLETON | 1873 ⊗ Daisy SINGLETON | 1876 ⊗ Susannah SINGLETON | 1858 - 1957 ⊠ 99 Arthur FRANKLAND | 1872 - 1966 ⊗ 94 Ada Emma SINGLETON | 1874 ⊠ John SINGLETON | 1877 ⊠ George SINGLETON | 1880 ⊗ Alice SINGLETON | ⊗ Phoebe M SINGLETON |

m. Wandsworth, London 1897

| 1894 ⊠ Ernest George FRANKLAND | 1898 ⊠ Reginald Arthur FRANKLAND | 1899 ⊠ Leslie Arthur John FRANKLAND | 1904 - 1997 ⊗ 93 Irene Cooper FRANKLAND | 1906 - 1941 ⊗ 35 Muriel Neech FRANKLAND | 1907 - 2005 ⊗ / ⊠ 98 Roy Evelyn FRANKLAND |

From the early 18th century, the Singletons were born and lived in Richmond, Surrey. The most common names being Miles and George. George was indeed the given name for my 3xG Grandfather, born in 1791. George married Mary Springall who was considerably younger, born in 1807. They had three sons, George, Charles and John (possibly named after his maternal grandfather). George was a shoemaker, or perhaps only a cobbler, for he was certainly impecunious, and left his family in very straitened circumstances. Sylvia writes that he seems to have been a serious man. Apart from being a strict Nonconformist, he had a liking for poetry, and used to read Shakespeare, as well as the Bible, with his wife.

[Jealousy, was said to be his great fault, and if he even so much as dreamt that his wife Mary had spoken to another man, he would not speak to her the next day. Apparently, once, after a particularly vivid dream, he did not speak for a whole week. Finally, thoroughly weary of the situation, his wife, who was a spirited young woman, hit on a possible solution. Suddenly, she started to rummage through drawers and cupboards, throwing the contents on to the floor, until his curiosity was too much for him. He asked whatever was she looking for? 'I've found it! I've found it!' she cried. 'What?' 'Your tongue!'] *[Sylvia]*

Their middle son, Charles, died aged just 13, in 1854. Two years later, George died without warning, when his youngest son John was 10 years old.

[He carried John upstairs one night, sat down on the bed, and died. There was no poor relief, other than that given in the workhouse, so the family was plunged into extreme poverty. They succeeded nevertheless, it seems, to maintain an unblemished respectability. The elder son George had just completed his apprenticeship as a tailor. His small earnings as a journeyman were all the family had to live on. His mother is said to have gone without food to ensure that the breadwinner should have enough nourishment.]

[Sylvia]

It is perhaps not surprising then that 3x Great Uncle George developed a strong sense of the importance of money.

Mary Singleton (nee Springall)

Mary Singleton, born Springall, was, according to accounts heard by Sylvia, a 'woman of character with a sharp and sometimes sarcastic tongue'. When Sylvia was growing up, her grandmother Ada would sometimes show signs of a similar liveliness of wit and the family would say that she had inherited 'the Springall sarcasm'.

[Her life after her husband's death must have often been frustrating, and in spite of the problem of jealousy, she must have missed the mild intellectualism which had led to poetry readings. Her daughters-in-law, two sisters called Neech, in one or other of whose households she spent the last years of her life, were good, pious young women with no intellectual leanings whatever.]
[Sylvia]

After her son George married Pheobe Neech, Mary lived with them and their growing family for a number of years. She helped with his tailoring business whenever there was a busy period. It was George's practice to press his mother and daughters Rosa, Phoebe, Daisy and Susie (as soon as they were old enough) into helping at those times. All four girls became expert buttonholers from when they were quite young. When age prevented Mary from these activities, she was sent to live with her younger son John and his wife Rebecca.

[In those days, before widows' pensions, the complete dependence of a penniless widow, like Mary Singleton, on the charity of her children must have been a humiliating burden to bear, especially if the children themselves were far from prosperous. She seems to have been very conscious of it, and apparently never liked her granddaughter Ada because the little girl, fascinated by the way her grandmother's neck moved up and down when she chewed, used to watch her at meal times. The hyper-sensitive old lady thought the child begrudged her every mouthful she ate. She was perhaps touchy through frustration in any case and not always easy to live with, but in later years her daughter-in-law Rebecca, in her own old age, said: 'I could have been kinder and more considerate to her'. Thus, we understand life backwards. Although she was not fond of Ada, she loved her other grandchildren, especially Johnny, the younger of her two grandsons.

A great many poor, but intelligent Victorian women must have led similarly hard and restricted lives.]
[Sylvia]

The brothers, George and John, had married two sisters, Phoebe and Rebecca, but their households were reported to be very different. George and Phoebe's home was in Richmond and *'was improvident and cheerful, casual and somewhat slapdash'*. George's income could be sporadic. Times of prosperity would be accompanied by extravagance, including finery for his wife and daughters and wasted food. This shocked Rebecca, who was a methodical and careful housewife. John's income however, as a wine merchant, came in regular weekly amounts, unlike his brother's.

George Singleton and Phoebe Neech

[George, ten years older than his brother John, was a good-looking and at least superficially attractive man, as a photograph taken with Phoebe during their engagement bears out.]

[Sylvia]
Sylvia writes that her father Ernest was said to resemble George and did not relish this comparison.

[Apart from the four daughters, there was one son, Charles, who also became a tailor. Phoebe died painfully in middle age of an internal cancer, inexpertly nursed by her young daughters, and George subsequently remarried. His choice of a second wife seems to have been largely dictated by the lady's being a widow with money, but with this she proved to be extremely mean, and he had a very thin time. She was unpopular with her step-children who always called her 'The Mater'. He did not survive her and she went on the marry yet another unwary man.

George's four daughters all married. The eldest, Rosa, was an elegant, proud girl who became engaged to an attractive young man called Nathaniel Redding, a skilled carver by trade. She committed the unforgiveable sin for a girl in a Victorian Nonconformist family of becoming pregnant before the wedding. The shame of this was too much for her, and shortly after they were married the young couple emigrated to Australia, where Nathaniel had been promised a good job through an advertisement. On arrival, however, he found that there was no job. His correspondent, having been deceived himself over promised work, had decided to play the same trick on someone else. As a result, their early days were a great struggle; Nathaniel was forced to work on the roads as a labourer, but in time they made good, and had a family of one son and several daughters. The son, also Nathaniel, was killed in the first War. He was said to have enlisted in the Anzac Brigade because he was fascinated by the photograph of one of his English cousins, Lily Singleton, and hoped for an opportunity to meet her. They did indeed meet, when he was on leave, and even got engaged, but he was killed soon afterwards and contact with his family was lost.

Rosa and Nathaniel Redding with their son and 3 daughters

Daisy Eggleton (nee Singleton) with granddaughter Marguerite

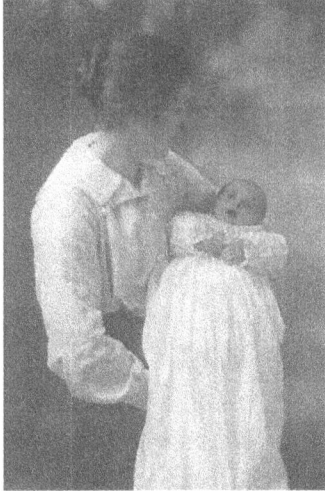

Another sister, Daisy, married a very short man named Frederick Eggleton. As she was rather tall, she always walked with a stoop to minimise the difference in height. She and her family emigrated to Australia after the first War, when her eldest daughter Winnie, a pretty, affected and very flirtatious girl, married an Australian soldier, Frank Westbrook.'

Frank Westbrook wrote a small book of poems called 'Anzac and After' of which we have a copy. In it, Frank wrote about Australia and his war-time experiences. Despite taking part at Gallipoli and losing many friends, it appears that his attitude to the war remained unquestioning.] [Sylvia]

Frank Westbrook, cover photograph from

'Anzac and After'

This, one of 34 poems in Frank Westbrook's book, was written in London, in March 1916

Why?
Why did I go to the wars? "Dunno."
No doubt it was destiny forced me to go,
I had dashed little knowledge of national things
Pertaining to treaties and statutes and kings;
A hazy idea that a 'ell of a scrap
Was twisting and changing the tints on a map;
Grim tellings of slaughter and terrible shame,
And capping them all was Germany's name;
Of fates worse than death for a mother and maid,
Perhaps through it all I was somewhat afraid
When remembering those who are dearer to me
Than my life. And yes, there may be
In the thoughts of their honour an impelling spur
To make things quite sure for my mother and Her.
Perhaps 'twas some writer or speaker I'd heard,
The blood of my ancestors waken and stirred,
And flung to my brain an appeal to my breed.
Mayhap I followed some other chap's lead.
Or was the natural love of a scrap
Some sort of daredevil that wakes in a chap,
That challenges death for a jest or a taunt,
The sheer joy of living that nothing will daunt.
I dunno, but I've fought and I've been through the mill.
What made me a soldier's a mystery still;
But home's not a home if it's not worth a fight-
All things put together I know I've done right.
Through danger and dark days and death I am here,
I'm not learned or clever, but one thing is clear,
I've a lot to be lost and dern little to gain,
But if things were reversed I'd just do it again;
For I know (for I've been) that war is just hell,
Where death lurks with vermin and noise and foul smell,
But all things considered I'd go out once more,
Though I'll never know rightly what takes me to war.

Winnie and Frank Westbrook's wedding - March 1918

Daisy and Fred Eggleton are on the right of the photograph.

Daisy had four children. Winnie, George, Cecil and Muriel. We are now happily in contact with Cecil's son and Muriel's daughter who are also keen researchers of our ancestors.

The voyage out to Australia at that time took at least six weeks. For impecunious emigrants it was necessarily a departure for life. Ada and Daisy exchanged letters for the rest of Daisy's life, and she reported bouts of homesickness especially when news arrived from England.

One of her letters to Ada, kept safely by Sylvia, starts;

Dear Ada and everybody,

We were all delighted to get your bright, newsy letter this morning, just before Fred left for town. I could hardly stop to see him off before reading it. Then Muriel and I talked, oh how we talked, until long after Esther had gone to school. How near you brought everyone and how homesick I felt. I very much fear I shall never come back again, but we'll all meet again in the 'Glory Land'.

And ends;

My dearest love to Auntie. I would love to talk to her. Though Fred says now my hair is white, I am the living image of her. I wish I were as good too. Tell everyone I send love too and especially to you and Arthur. Your very affectionate cousins Daisy and Fred.

Charles Singleton, the only son of George and Phoebe married a young woman called Ada Green. They lived in what was reported to be a beautifully maintained home at Penge. As already stated, Charles was also a tailor by profession. Within the family they were always referred to as 'The Penge Folk'.

John Singleton	Rebecca Singleton (nee Neech)

Family recollection is that John Singleton, my 2xG Grandfather, was quite different in temperament to his brother George. He was a mild, deeply pious man, who was devoted to his wife Rebecca and his family. His main sources of relaxation were gardening and fishing. His son-in-law, Arthur Frankland, thought it ridiculous that he should rise early every day, before going to work, to water his patch of garden. Family holidays could also be particularly embarrassing, as John insisted on lying his fishing rods flat across the seats of the train, regardless of the indignant looks of other passengers. The destination for holidays was always Beccles, in Suffolk, where the family stayed with Rebecca's father Samuel Neech. Samuel and John would then enjoy time fishing in the River Waveney.

Sylvia recalls her father Ernest saying of John; *'He was clumsy in the most practical things 'to see him trying to mend something was to think he was trying to break it.'*

[The poverty into which the family was plunged by the death of their father, meant that he had little formal education, but he inherited a liking for serious things, including poetry, and was much given to quoting from the 18th century poet Dr Edward Young, whose gloomy series of 'Night Thoughts' enjoyed a considerable vogue for many years. Two lines which were particular favourites passed into family usage and were still being quoted in my (Sylvia's) own childhood, long after his death.

'Tired. Nature's sweet restorer, balmy sleep' – was considered appropriate for juveniles reluctant to go 'up the wooden hill and down sheet lane,' while

'Procrastination is the thief of Time' – was useful as a reproach to the dilatory.

Other quotations tended to be biblical, a favourite being from St John's Gospel: 'Men love darkness better than light because their deeds are evil.'] [Sylvia]

John kept scrap books for many years, keeping items that interested him from newspapers or magazines. He was also fascinated by phrenology (the study of the size and shape of the cranium as a supposed indicator of character and mental faculties). At the time, this was regarded as scientific. John's use of the technique would be referred to as 'Grandpa reading your bumps'. Apparently, all of his grandchildren were subjected to the assessment, but no diagnosis was ever given, just a knowing smile.

At the age of 76, John suffered a stroke which left him partially paralysed. Unfortunately, he was left bedridden for the remaining two years of his life.

[He was devotedly nursed by his wife, and lived mainly on bread and milk, then considered an ideal invalid food. His grand-daughters Irene and Marjorie Frankland and Doris Holton, used to go and read to him after school: he seems to have borne his disabilities with exemplary patience. 'I never heard him say a cross word,' Doris said many years later.] [Sylvia]

John died in 1923.

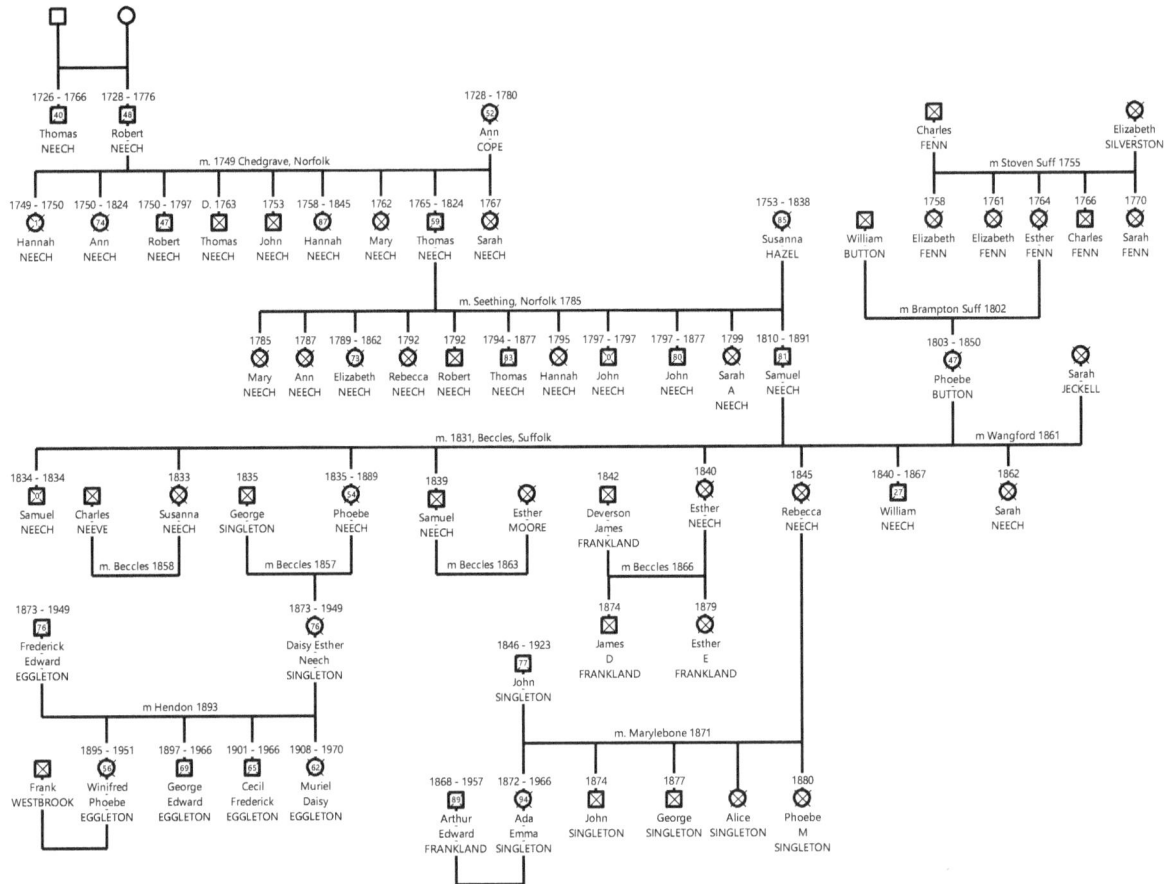

Family tree — The Neeches

- ☐ — ◯
- 1726 - 1766 Thomas NEECH [40]
- 1728 - 1776 Robert NEECH [48]
- 1728 - 1780 Ann COPE [52]

m. 1749 Chedgrave, Norfolk

- 1749 - 1750 Hannah NEECH
- 1750 - 1824 Ann NEECH [74]
- 1750 - 1797 Robert NEECH [47]
- D. 1763 Thomas NEECH
- 1753 John NEECH
- 1758 - 1845 Hannah NEECH [07]
- 1762 Mary NEECH
- 1765 - 1824 Thomas NEECH [59]
- 1767 Sarah NEECH
- 1753 - 1838 Susanna HAZEL [83]
- Charles FENN
- Elizabeth SILVERSTON

m Stoven Suff 1755

- 1758 William BUTTON
- 1758 Elizabeth FENN
- 1761 Elizabeth FENN
- 1764 Esther FENN
- 1766 Charles FENN
- 1770 Sarah FENN

m. Seething, Norfolk 1785

- 1785 Mary NEECH
- 1787 Ann NEECH
- 1789 - 1862 Elizabeth NEECH
- 1792 Rebecca NEECH
- 1792 Robert NEECH
- 1794 - 1877 Thomas NEECH [93]
- 1795 Hannah NEECH
- 1797 - 1797 John NEECH
- 1797 - 1877 John NEECH [80]
- 1799 Sarah A NEECH
- 1810 - 1891 Samuel NEECH [81]

m Brampton Suff 1802

- 1803 - 1850 Phoebe BUTTON [47]
- Sarah JECKELL

m Wangford 1861

m. 1831, Beccles, Suffolk

- 1834 - 1834 Samuel NEECH
- 1833 Charles NEEVE
- 1833 Susanna NEECH
- 1835 George SINGLETON
- 1835 - 1889 Phoebe NEECH
- 1839 Samuel NEECH
- Esther MOORE
- 1842 Deverson James FRANKLAND
- 1840 Esther NEECH
- 1845 Rebecca NEECH
- 1840 - 1867 William NEECH
- 1862 Sarah NEECH

m. Beccles 1858 — m Beccles 1857 — m Beccles 1863 — m Beccles 1866

- 1873 - 1949 Frederick Edward EGGLETON [76]
- 1873 - 1949 Daisy Esther Neech SINGLETON [79]
- 1846 - 1923 John SINGLETON [77]
- 1874 James D FRANKLAND
- 1879 Esther E FRANKLAND

m Hendon 1893

m. Marylebone 1871

- 1895 - 1951 Frank WESTBROOK
- 1897 - 1966 Winifred Phoebe EGGLETON [69]
- 1901 - 1966 George Edward EGGLETON [65]
- 1908 - 1970 Cecil Frederick EGGLETON
- Muriel Daisy EGGLETON
- 1868 - 1957 Arthur Edward FRANKLAND [80]
- 1872 - 1966 Ada Emma SINGLETON
- 1874 John SINGLETON
- 1877 George SINGLETON
- 1880 Alice SINGLETON
- Phoebe M SINGLETON

George and John Singleton then, married two sisters from Suffolk, Phoebe and Rebecca Neech. The Neech family background appears quite different to the Singletons. The Neech family during the 16th and 17th centuries is found in the area centred on Mendham, in the Waveney Valley. There was little movement during this time, probably due to them being land owners. In their wills, most of the men were described as yeomen and there is evidence of considerable wealth in land, property and money. By the end of the 17th century, the family was vast, covering South Norfolk as well as North Suffolk.

They lived in an area known for its dairies, an area of agricultural prosperity in the 16th and 17th centuries with a high proportion of yeomen and small freeholders. In an article written by Nesta Evans, she suggests that the rural economy of the Waveney Valley, based on dairying and hemp growing, was such that small acreages were viable and able to provide a better living than was the case in the arable areas of Suffolk.

At some stage in this period of relative affluence, they acquired a coat of arms: 'Neech of Mendham' being listed in the 17th century Visitations. The description is

'A paly of six argent and sable per gess counterchanged'.

In line with the religious tendencies of 17th century Suffolk, the Neeches had leanings towards Puritanism.

Certainties for our family, begin with Robert Neech who was born in 1728. Robert married Ann Cope in Chedgrave, Norfolk in 1749 and they went on to have nine children. Two of the children, Hannah and Thomas, are known to have died in infancy. Subsequently, the second youngest, born in 1765, was again named Thomas and it is this Thomas who is my 4xG Grandfather.

Thomas's own marriage to Susanna Hazel is recorded in the parish records in 1785, as are the baptisms of their eleven children, between 1785 and 1801. They arrived at roughly 18-month intervals: Mary, Ann, Elizabeth, Rebecca, Robert, Thomas, Hannah and John (who died in infancy), another John, Sarah and Samuel. There seems to have been another son also, but not baptised in Beccles, for an Edmund Hazel Neech occurs in the 1845 edition of 'White's Directory of Norfolk' as a pilot at King's Lynn. The names Robert, Thomas, John and Edmund occur regularly in the families of the earlier Mendham group of Neeches. Samuel, although being used in more than one 19th century generation, does not appear to have been used earlier. It is Samuel who is our direct ancestor.

Neeches Yard – today, still called the same

Apart from the seafaring Edmund, the Neeches were still involved in agricultural pursuits. Samuel Neech is entered in White's Directories for 1844 and 1874 as a cattle dealer of Ravens Moor, Beccles. He is also variously described as a cattle jobber and hay dealer in the Censuses for Beccles. Neeches Yard is still named as such in Fenn Lane, close to the River Waveney.

In 1831, when he was approaching thirty, Samuel married Phoebe Button the daughter of William Button and his wife Esther, nee Fenn. Between 1833 and 1846 they had seven children. The family was made up of three sons, two named Samuel (one of whom died in infancy) and the other William and four daughters, Susanna, Phoebe, Esther and Rebecca, my 2xG Grandmother. Typically, they were named after members of the family, Samuel after his father, William after his maternal grandfather, Susanna after her paternal grandmother, Phoebe after her mother and Esther after her maternal grandmother. The names are biblical in origin and Sylvia writes that Samuel was a severe and deeply religious man. Samuel himself was baptised in the local parish church, but he seems to have become a Dissenter at an early stage and none of the children were baptised. On the day of the 1871 Census for Beccles a Nonconformist minister was staying in the house. The children's dates of birth were all kept in a 'birthday book' kept by Ada and Arthur Frankland.

There is not much information about my 3xG Grandfather Samuel Neech, except that passed on by his youngest daughter, Rebecca. She was only five when her mother died, and from an early age she kept house for her father, her older sisters being away.

[Samuel was very strict with his daughters, who particularly remembered (and no doubt resented) his not allowing them artificial flowers in their hats, saying that if they wanted adornment there were plenty of flowers growing in the hedgerows. He also had the reputation locally of being mean, although it was said in his defence that this was simply necessary carefulness because he had to support the family of a deceased brother as well as his own. His supposed meanness did not pass on to his daughters, however, and one of them – probably Esther – was willing to give her plate of dinner to any beggar who called at the right moment. Samuel's other notable talent was that he sang counter-tenor.

It is not easy to form much idea of what Phoebe Neech was like, and there is no photograph of her. In those days of haphazard amateur nursing she was in demand from neighbours as a midwife, and feeling that she was being imposed upon, her husband took her and the family away from Beccles for a time. It appears that she was meek, but kindly, and she was reputedly 'a delicate woman all her life' who miscarried very easily. She certainly reacted in true Victorian fashion in the one episode which has come down to us. One of the daughters was such a late talker that, when by the age of four she had never said a word, her parents came to the conclusion that she would always be dumb, something they were prepared to accept as the will of God. However, one day when she was in the garden a cheeky boy pulled at her skirt through the bars of the gate and the indignant little girl said quite clearly 'I'll tell my mother!' whereupon her mother promptly fainted.] [Sylvia]

As Rebecca was so young when her mother died, family stories often came via her older sisters. These included romanticised accounts about escaping from France that appear to have no historical basis. One recollection, however, did prove to be true. This was the story that Thomas Neech, Rebecca's uncle was transported to Australia for seven years following a conviction for sheep-stealing. A newspaper account left little doubt that he and his accomplice were guilty, but the family always declared his innocence, and were convinced that the sheep had been deliberately planted on his land. The event occurred in 1835, as reported:

'Thomas Neech & Andrew Turner of Willingham were indicted on the 29th June at Beccles for stealing two sheep the property of Mr Gibson of Willingham. It appears that they were ewes. Acquitted but remanded to the Ipswich Sessions.'

They were tried at the Ipswich Quarter Sessions on 3rd July 1835, convicted on the same charge and transported for life.

Beccles court and Gaol House was where they were held prior to transportation.

The photograph was taken as it was being demolished, many years later.

Thomas sailed on the 'Strathfieldsaye' on 11th February 1836 along with 270 other convicts, bound for New South Wales. Although transported for life, he was said to have returned on completion of his seven-year sentence, but on finding that his wife had in the meantime married someone else, he returned to Australia and was never heard of again.

[In spite of her father's sternness, Rebecca was very happy at home where the absence of other women gave her a certain amount of extra freedom in the household. On one occasion when she was a child she paid a visit to relations and on her return several days later went around kissing all the furniture because she was so pleased to be back. There were always animals about, and once she was warned particularly not to go near a pony which was said to be vicious. Being very small she did not heed the warning and when she offered the pony a handful of fodder it bit off her thumb with the hay, leaving it hanging by the skin. Her father had to travel ten miles with her to the nearest doctor. The thumb was saved, but the doctor sewed it on again the wrong way around, and so it stayed for the rest of her life.

The household was deeply religious and Calvinistic and Rebecca was much exercised in her teens to know whether she was one of the Elect. One day she prayed most earnestly for some sign of whether this was so, and the whole day passed without any response. By bedtime she had come to the conclusion that there was no hope for her, but as she went dolefully upstairs she was filled with a sudden joy, which convinced her that she was saved after all. This story she told all her life and it was known to her grandchildren (quite erroneously) as 'Grandma's conversion'. Fortunately, the family, although continuing to be deeply religious, ceased to hold the pernicious doctrines of Calvin by the turn of the century.]
[Sylvia]

Samuel Neech married Sarah Jeckell in 1861, when Rebecca was 16. The thought of having a step mother did not appeal to her and she promptly left home and went to London, where her sister Phoebe was married to George Singleton and her sister Esther to James (Deverson) Frankland. Like most Victorian girls, she was only experienced in domestic affairs and so she went into service, with a magistrate's family. Joseph Turnley, who was now blind and his wife Mary Ann were both elderly. They lived at 5, Sutherland Gardens in Paddington and Rebecca became one of their three servants. After being her own mistress from an early age, this change cannot have been altogether welcome, but was evidently preferable to life with a stepmother. Her father, Samuel, and his new wife Sarah, went on to have another daughter, Sarah Neech, in 1862.

[Before she went to London she was courted by Robert Frankland, the sandy-haired younger son of William Frankland, a harness-maker and saddler of Beccles. Rebecca told him firmly that she 'didn't like him and never would', and rebuffed he tried his luck elsewhere, marrying while still very young, a self-willed young woman called Priscilla Cooper. They produced a family of ten children of whom four (two sets of twin girls) died in infancy. Their sons were John, Arthur, James, William, Walter and Henry.]
[Sylvia]
In the course of time Arthur Frankland became my Great Grandfather.

Rebecca, on arrival in London, met and subsequently married John Singleton, the younger brother of her brother-in-law George.

[Her employers, who seem to have had some regard for her, gave her as wedding presents two fine cut glass salt cellars, four matching balloon-back chairs in an elegant Regency design and a pretty little sofa with a single raised end. By the 1870s all these items, charming though they were, had become out of date and unfashionable, and no doubt their owners were pleased to pass them on to grateful recipients. The chairs were said to be the survivors of a set of twelve. These gifts I'm sure were typical of the way Victorian employers got rid of unwanted household items on their servants and were able to appear generous in the process. The chairs and the salt cellars have now come down to me, and so

have remained in the family for more than one hundred and thirty years. The sofa, to my sorrow, was given away and lost. Rebecca also inherited from her eldest sister, Susanna, four black and white Spode dessert plates and two matching oval serving dishes. These must have been the surviving elements of a larger service simply given away. Today the four plates and one serving dish hang on our dining room wall.]   *[Sylvia]*

John and Rebecca had five children: Ada, George, John, Alice, who died in infancy and Phoebe.

[Rebecca was staying with her sister Phoebe in Richmond not long before her first child, Ada, was due and she unexpectedly went into labour there. The birth was appallingly mismanaged, with no doctor or midwife in attendance, and Rebecca suffered from the effects of it for the rest of her life. It is indicative of George Singleton's curious sense of humour that, when he wrote to his brother to tell him he had a fine daughter, John thought he was joking and took no notice for several days.]
[Sylvia]

When John and Rebecca were first married, they lived with her sister and brother-in-law, Esther and James (Deverson) Frankland at 95, Sabine Road Battersea. James was a class leader and local preacher in the Lavender Hill circuit of the Primitive Methodists. 'The Christian Messenger' states:

'He has the gift of ready utterance, speaks plain Saxon speech, and is thus heard and understood by the people. He is largely a man of one book – the Bible. It is his daily companion. His sermons and advice are full of apt scriptural quotations.'

Deverson James Frankland (James)

James was a very stern and pious man.

[The household was strictly Sabbatarian: no toys were allowed on Sundays, even if it happened to be Christmas Day. Ada could remember one Christmas when she was about five. She had been given a little wicker doll's pram which she longed to play with. Knowing that Uncle James would not approve, she wheeled it stealthily in the hall, and fortunately he never found out this outrageous example of Sabbath-breaking.]   *[Sylvia]*

At this time there was a shortage of small houses in London that would be suitable for poor families. The renting of larger houses, that were then occupied by a number of families, became commonplace.

In the 1860s the problem began to be tackled, with the building of small terraced houses. In Battersea, the Shaftsbury Estate was built on sloping ground near the railway line which ran from Clapham Junction to Victoria.

It was there, to 205, Eversleigh Road, that Rebecca moved with her husband John, in about 1878. The estate was named after Lord Shaftesbury, a great 19th century philanthropist, who championed the rights of working people to have adequate housing.

[The estate was a model of correctness and decorum. Those who failed to pay their rent regularly were promptly given notice. No rowdiness was tolerated and above all there were no public houses to lower the tone. This was in complete contrast to Culvert Road, on the other side of the railway lines, where the houses were interspersed with several public houses and things could get very rowdy indeed, especially on a Saturday night.]   *[Sylvia]*

Rebecca's grandson Ernest would tell his daughter that women had been known to fight with hatpins! Years later, when the unruly days had passed, the family would continue to use the area as a yardstick of undesirable behaviour. 'Stop behaving like Culvert Road,' being a severe rebuke.

[Eversleigh Road was a tree-lined street of little terraced houses at the very bottom of the Estate, low-lying and abutting directly on the railway, which ran just beyond the brick walls at the end of the small gardens. The noise of passing trains, frequent during the day and never entirely ceasing at night, punctuates every memory of 205. There are still one or two people in the family who remember it fondly, for this small dwelling, identical to all the others in the street, belonged to a succession of our relations for nearly a century.

205, Eversleigh Road – as it is today

There were no front gardens, only a strip of concrete and a row of ornate railings: brick gateposts, but no gate that I can remember. A minute path led to the front door, with a raised doorstep which was regularly washed and whitened. The front of the house was really rather ugly, built of London stock bricks of a greyish-yellow with some red brick decoration. The adjacent entrance doors of each pair of houses were under one peaked gable roof. There were flat sash windows without glazing-bars, and a slate roof. But they were solidly built and withstood the vibrations of the passing trains well. The nearest station was at Clapham Junction, one of the busiest stations in the country, serving the south coast and a series of suburban stations south of London. Several lines passed the houses, some on the same low level and others further away, raised. Between the lower and the upper lines was a sort of no man's land, uncomfortably inhabited by a troop of gypsies in brightly painted caravans. From time to time they came on to the Estate selling dolly-pegs and telling fortunes.

The entrance hall led into a narrow passage with the stairs at the end and the living room doors to one side. The two living rooms were of equal size, but that facing the street, known simply at 205 as 'the front room', was kept for best and only used on special occasions. This was a pity since only the front room of the house got any sunshine: the back faced north, but it was in the dark kitchen-cum-living room and the equally dark scullery behind it that most of the life of the household went on. Cooking was done on the black range in the kitchen, washing in the copper in the corner of the scullery, which had the only water tap in the whole house. Hot water for tea or cooking was heated by an enormous kettle in the kitchen, larger amounts were boiled in the copper. Baths were taken in a galvanised bath in front of the kitchen range, a cosy proceeding which I remember from my youth. But, by the time I was not much more than five, the range had been modernised away and replaced by an open fire, and the cooking had shifted to a gas stove in the scullery.

The kitchen window looked out onto part of the tiny walled garden which had one of the railway lines running immediately beyond it. The scullery and the room above it were in a small rear wing, narrower and lower than the rest of the house, and at a later stage, but before my time, a glazed outhouse was built beyond it. This my grandfather turned into a workshop for his woodwork and he always called it simply 'the shop'. He was a very gifted carpenter and joiner and made much of the furniture in the house: my recollection of 'the shop' is of the lovely smell of newly-sawn wood and the curls of wood shavings which appeared as he planed. Later still, this area became a bathroom.

The stairs were dark and narrow, leading to a minute half-landing with the room over the scullery leading off it. This was called 'the ante room'. Above it the stairs turned in a sharp curve towards the unlighted main landing, also very small. To one side was the back bedroom, over the kitchen; in front was the main bedroom, which, because it was over the passage as well as the room below, was the largest room in the house. The plan of these small dwellings was based on that of the much larger town houses built in the Georgian period, although they would also have had a half basement and a second upper story, and the large upper room of the first floor was intended to be the drawing room. In the cut down version of the plan found on the Shaftesbury Estate this was not feasible and the upper front room became the principle bedroom. The additional width of the room was no doubt often welcome, for Victorian families were large and the parents slept with cots and beds for some of the children in their room.]   *[Sylvia]*

This was then, the house where Rebecca and John Singleton lived for many years and in which their children Ada, George, John and Phoebe grew up.

[Another little girl called Alice came between John and Phoebe but lived only about two years. Johnnie, as he was always called, was very jealous of his younger sister and never wanted her to come back, but Rebecca was much saddened by the loss of her child.

From time to time they were visited by Rebecca's father, Samuel Neech. Ada remembered his visits when, in his presence, she would play very quietly and never utter a word. She was in many ways a timid child and Victorian grandfathers were formidable people. She did not mention her reaction to her other grandfather, Robert Frankland, but he also came to visit on occasion, claiming that his youthful love for Rebecca had never dimmed.]   *[Sylvia]*

Rebecca and John left the house sometime between 1901 and 1911 and moved in with Robert's sister Emma Riddington (nee Frankland) who lived with her daughter, Emma Elizabeth, following the death of her husband David. 205, Eversleigh Road then became home to their daughter Ada.

The Coopers

1725 - 1785
Samuel COOPER

1725
Elizabeth

m Coombs 1764

1750 - 1820
James COOPER

1755 - 1825
Martha MAYES

1742 - 1812
Isaac CLARK

Ann ROSE

m Sth Elmham 1775

m Bradfield St Clare Suffolk 1764

1764 - 1841
Jonathan COOPER

1765 - 1801
Samuel COOPER

1777 - 1856
James COOPER

1765
Elizabeth CLARK

1766
Charlotte CLARK

1768
Isaac CLARK

1769
Susanna CLARK

1771
William CLARK

1773
Jabez CLARK

1776 - 1833
Priscilla CLARK

1777
Ann CLARK

1780
Sarah CLARK

1787
Meriah CLARK

William VINCE

Elizabeth

Michael KNIGHTS

Susanna BIRKETT

m Beccles 1814

, Kettlebaston Suffolk 1798

1800 - 1871
Priscilla COOPER

1803 - 1888
James COOPER

1804
Maria COOPER

1806
Thomas COOPER

1807
Samuel COOPER

1809 - 1893
Jonathan COOPER

1811
Phoebe COOPER

1815 - 1879
John COOPER

1818
Ebenezer COOPER

1807 - 1858
Elizabeth Mary Jones VINCE

1816
Matilda VINCE

1821
Adam VINCE

1815
Susan KNIGHTS

1819
Anne KNIGHTS

1817
George KNIGHTS

1817
Susan KNIGHTS

5 more siblings

1816
Hannah Marie WOOLNER

m. St Martin in the Fields 1841

m Wangford 1860

m Kessingland, Suffolk 1842

1844 - 1926
Robert FRANKLAND

1843 - 1877
Priscilla COOPER

1845 - 1915
Jemima COOPER

1844
Hannah Maria KNIGHTS

1845
George KNIGHTS

1846
Frederick KNIGHTS

1848
Edward KNIGHTS

1851
Mary Ann KNIGHTS

m. Stowmarket, Beccles, Suffolk 1863

m Beccles 1879

1866
John Cooper FRANKLAND

1868 - 1957
Arthur Edward FRANKLAND

1870
James Bareham FRANKLAND

1872
Walter Robert FRANKLAND

1873
William Joseph FRANKLAND

1875
Henry Albert FRANKLAND

1876 - 1876
Ellen Priscilla FRANKLAND

1881
Ellen (Nellie) Julia FRANKLAND

1883
Alice Ruth FRANKLAND

1884
Frederick Charles FRANKLAND

1887
Millicent Marion Elizabeth FRANKLAND

1872 - 1966
Ada Emma SINGLETON

The earliest Coopers were based between Bury St Edmonds and Ipswich, in Suffolk, at Coombs, Bradfield St Clare and Kettlebaston. They were Nonconformists and worshipped at Wattisham Strict Baptist Chapel, founded in 1763. The Strict Baptists or Particular Baptists were a breakaway group formed in about 1633 believing in 'Particular Atonement', theology closely aligned to Calvinism. The Toleration Act of 1689, relaxed the restriction on nonconformists and the Particular Baptists became the main form of Baptism. Baptists do not christen their children, but do record their births in the chapel records, which are available online and are extremely useful for family research. The children were invariably given names taken from the Bible. In our Cooper family, Jonathan, Samuel and James were the names of choice for boys.

James and Martha Cooper had three sons, as might be predicted, these were Jonathan, Samuel and James. The youngest, James, was born in 1777. He married Priscilla Clark, the daughter of Isaac and Ann Clark (nee Rose), in 1798. Priscilla was one of ten children, seven girls and three boys whose names included Jabez and Meriah. James and Priscilla, also had a large family of nine children: Priscilla, James, Maria, Thomas, Samuel, Johnathan, Phoebe, John and Ebenezer. James farmed at Charles Hall, Ringshall (the parish of his birth), near Stowmarket. The Coopers had been farming at Charles Hall for some time and continued to farm there at least until the end of the 19th century.

Charles Hall
Ringshall, near
Stowmarket

James and Priscilla's son John, my 3xG Grandfather, chose to become a miller. By the 1841 Census, he was already leasing a post-mill at Coombs and subsequently, he was tenant of a mill at Tunstall. John married Elizabeth Vince, at St Martin in the Fields, in 1841. Elizabeth was the daughter of a confectioner, based in London, although according to Census information, she was born in Dedham, just over the Suffolk boarder, in Essex.

John Cooper

Reminiscences of John are of a kindly man, who was perhaps a little too indulgent of Priscilla and Jemima, his two daughters. Sadly, their mother Elizabeth died in 1858, aged 51 years, leaving her two daughters aged 15 and 13 years.

At the time, they were living in the Rendham area, towards the east coast of Suffolk. The following year saw John moving a few miles north, to Beccles, where he purchased Ingate postmill on Ellough Road. This is described as, 'a substantial postmill with a flint roundhouse' and came up for sale following the death of the previous owner. Details about the mill are included in 'The Lost Windmills of Beccles', a Beccles Museum book.

A Portrait of John Cooper

In 1860, John remarried. His new wife was Anne Knights, a spinster born in Beccles and four years older than John. It seems likely that in the intervening years between the death of Elizabeth and John's marriage to Anne, the family were helped by John's eldest sister, Priscilla and her husband Daniel.

John's sister Priscilla had married Meshach Chaplin, the younger brother of Shadrach Chaplin (1786-1858), who was the 2xG Grandfather of one Charles Spencer Chaplin (1889-1977), more commonly known as "Charlie"! They had no children. Meshach Chaplin died in 1849 and in 1851 Priscilla was a widow and a farmer of 40 acres at Great Finborough. She married Daniel Bareham, from Essex, in Great Finborough, in 1851. Census returns show Daniel continued to farm the 40 acres until 1871, this was also the year of Priscilla's death. Daniel died in 1880. Daniel and Priscilla are the only Barehams that I have been able to trace.

Just before Priscilla's death, in 1869, Jemima Cooper, who had by then married Jonathan Lockwood, named her first born son John Bareham Lockwood. Shortly after this, in 1870, her sister Priscilla Cooper, who had by that time married Robert Frankland named her second son, James Bareham Frankland. This seems significant. Perhaps in that final chapter of Priscilla Bareham's life, both of John's daughters had decided to show their Aunt Priscilla how much she meant to them.

Priscilla Frankland (nee Cooper)

Priscilla and Robert had ten children between 1866 and 1876. Two sets of twin girls were among these. Three died at birth and one, Ellen Priscilla, just weeks after birth. Their six boys survived, among them my Great Grandfather, Arthur Edward Frankland, born in 1868. Sadly, Priscilla died just months after her second set of twin girls were born. She was 34 years old. Her death appears not to have been linked to her numerous pregnancies, but to something akin to Meningitis, which might have been easily treated today. Her death certificate states as cause of death;

'Cerebral congestion 10 days, cerebral effusion 6 days, convulsions 10 hours'

Her father, John, died no more than two years later, his death said to have been hastened by the loss of his child. Their graves are together in the Beccles Cemetery. There is a rather overgrown area, set at one end under trees, that is the area set aside for Nonconformists. John's second wife Anne is also there as well as another Cooper, whose first name and dates are illegible.

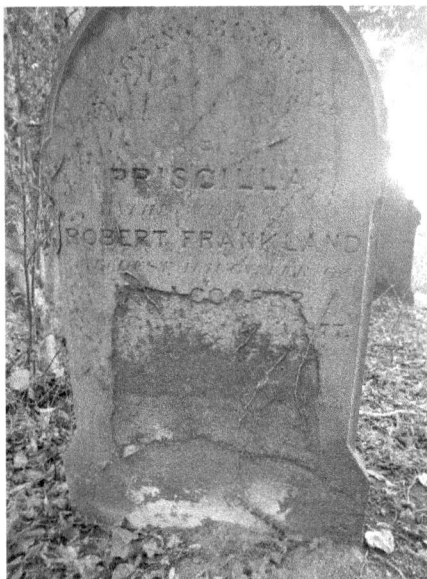

The Grave of Priscilla Frankland (nee Cooper)

The Grave of John Cooper

Beccles Cemetery, Non-Conformist Area, Showing the Cooper Family Graves

John died on 9th July 1879, at the age of 63 years. His Will was drawn up on 5th June 1879, with a codicil added on June 17th. It seems from the dates of the Will and his death that he was already ailing and realised that there was no time to lose. The Will was written in copperplate on parchment that is about a metre wide. He called himself 'gentleman', and although not a rich man, he owned shops in the New Market Place and Northgate Street as well as Ingate Mill.

John Cooper

To his wife Anne, he left his 'messuage in the London Road'. He gave instructions for the sale of the mill but retention of the other properties. These he vested in trustees, so that the revenue from them, together with the proceeds of the mill sale, could be paid to his wife and surviving daughter Jemima, as annuities. He also instructed that some of the proceeds of the sale of the mill should be invested 'in stocks of England or India' and used for 'the maintenance and education' of the children of his late daughter Priscilla Frankland. The wording relating to Jemima, suggests that her marriage was not satisfactory financially: she was given the money 'for her separate use, free from the debts and control of her husband'. It appears though, that John's bequest gave Jemima and her husband Jonathan Lockwood the security the family needed. They went on to have thirteen children, nine of whom survived infancy. In the 1911 Census return, the family home in Beccles still had a number of the now grown children living there, including the husband of Jemima's daughter Priscilla. Jemima died in 1915, two years after her husband.

Northgate Street, site of one of John's shops

The family home, 5, London Road, Beccles

[The money for the maintenance and education of John Cooper's grandsons was entrusted to his son-in-law, Robert Frankland, but sadly most of it was swallowed up in household expenses and very little of it went to education. I believe only two of the six boys went to the Sir John Leman Grammar School in Beccles; for the rest, including Arthur, it was only the local board school and their education ended when they were twelve. Even when the six boys were grown up, Robert continued to use the money he received as part of his own income, though since he was an unworldly man, I am sure it was not with any realisation that he was doing something wrong. By that time, he had another family growing up, and in the late 19th century times could be hard for rural craftsmen when agriculture was in a depressed state.

Arthur always remembered his grandfather with great affection, and his death, two years after Priscilla's, must have been an added trauma for the boy, who had adored his mother as well as being her confessed favourite. (Victorian mothers were quite able to say this sort of thing, horrifying as it is to a modern parent). As it was, he never really got over the loss of his mother, and his graphic description of how he learnt of her death could reduce me (Sylvia) to tears when he was an old man.

He had been staying away from home, in the nearby village of North Cove, possibly with relatives, as there was a substantial farmer named Cooper living there. Priscilla had just produced her 9th and 10th children, twin girls who did not long survive her. The sequence of events is not entirely clear to me: she did not die in childbirth but seems to have fallen fatally ill soon after the birth. Arthur was walking near North Cove when he met an itinerant pedlar who was known to him. The man immediately began to commiserate with him, 'You poor boy' over the loss of his mother and he cried out 'Is my mother dead?' not believing that it was true. He is said to have run all the way back to Beccles to find her. He was nine years old. A pall of darkness must have descended on him as he searched desperately; children cannot readily accept the finality of death.

The remainder of his childhood must have been bleak. His father, Robert, must have had a difficult task, caring for six little boys, the eldest not more than eleven, the youngest not even two. For a couple of years, they had an elderly housekeeper. Robert was not more than 31 when Priscilla died and, as someone with the uncomfortable combination of a passionate nature and strict religious beliefs, he was unlikely to remain a widower for long.]   *[Sylvia]*

Robert chose as his second wife, the niece of John's second wife, Hannah Knights, who had been a childhood friend of Priscilla's. According to Sylvia's recollections she was a 'refined and ladylike' young woman with no experience of running a household or looking after children. She was apparently reluctant to take on the task but agreed when she was told that the two eldest boys would be moving out of the family home quite soon (they were fourteen-year-old John and twelve-year-old Arthur). Indeed, they were married in 1879 and John Frankland had already moved out before the 1881 Census. They married very quietly, for it is recounted that the first the children knew of the wedding was when Robert ushered her into the room saying 'Well boys, here's your new mother'. Arthur was devastated and jumped up replying 'She's no mother of mine'. And so it was, that from the outset there was rather an explosive relationship between them.

[One cannot but have sympathy with Hannah, thrown into a situation which she doubtless found daunting. She rapidly became pregnant with her first child, a boy, who died shortly after birth. He was followed by four more births: three girls and another boy, named respectively Alice, Ellen, Frederick and Millicent. They were always referred to as 'the second family', and Arthur kept in touch with them sporadically as an adult.

Back row, left to right are:

Walter Robert Frankland
William Joseph Frankland
John Cooper Frankland
Arthur Edward Frankland
James Barham Frankland

Middle row, left to right:

Robert Frankland
Millicent Marion Elizabeth Frankland (baby)
Hannah Marie Frankland (nee Knights)
Henry Albert Frankland

Front row:

Alice Ruth Frankland
Frederick Charles Frankland
Ellen Julia Frankland

The Household of Arthur's youth must have been a grim and humourless place without Priscilla's lively presence and as cold and dark as most houses were at that time. Poor Hannah was an appalling cook, and the long-term digestive problems from which Arthur suffered all his life were doubtless related to this, and the subsequent feeding at the hands of his aunt Esther, equally hopeless. By the time he married, he was almost incapable of digesting anything.

Robert was a strong Calvinist and Sabbatarian and no cooking was allowed on Sundays at all, everything being prepared the night before. Most of Sunday was taken up by church services anyway. As a young man, in the days before church organs, Robert played the violin in church and he also had a good singing voice. (Priscilla had also been musical, and Arthur remembered all his life hearing her sing 'I Know That My Redeemer Liveth', from Handel's Messiah). At a later stage, Robert became a lay preacher in the Baptist church and spent all his Sundays driving around the countryside in a pony and trap, holding services in tiny village chapels. Arthur's son, Ernest, could remember accompanying him as a teenager, on his visits to Beccles.] *[Sylvia]*

Robert still visited Priscilla's family, indeed the 1911 Census records show him as a visitor of John Cooper, Priscilla's cousin, at Charles Hall in Stow.

The Franklands

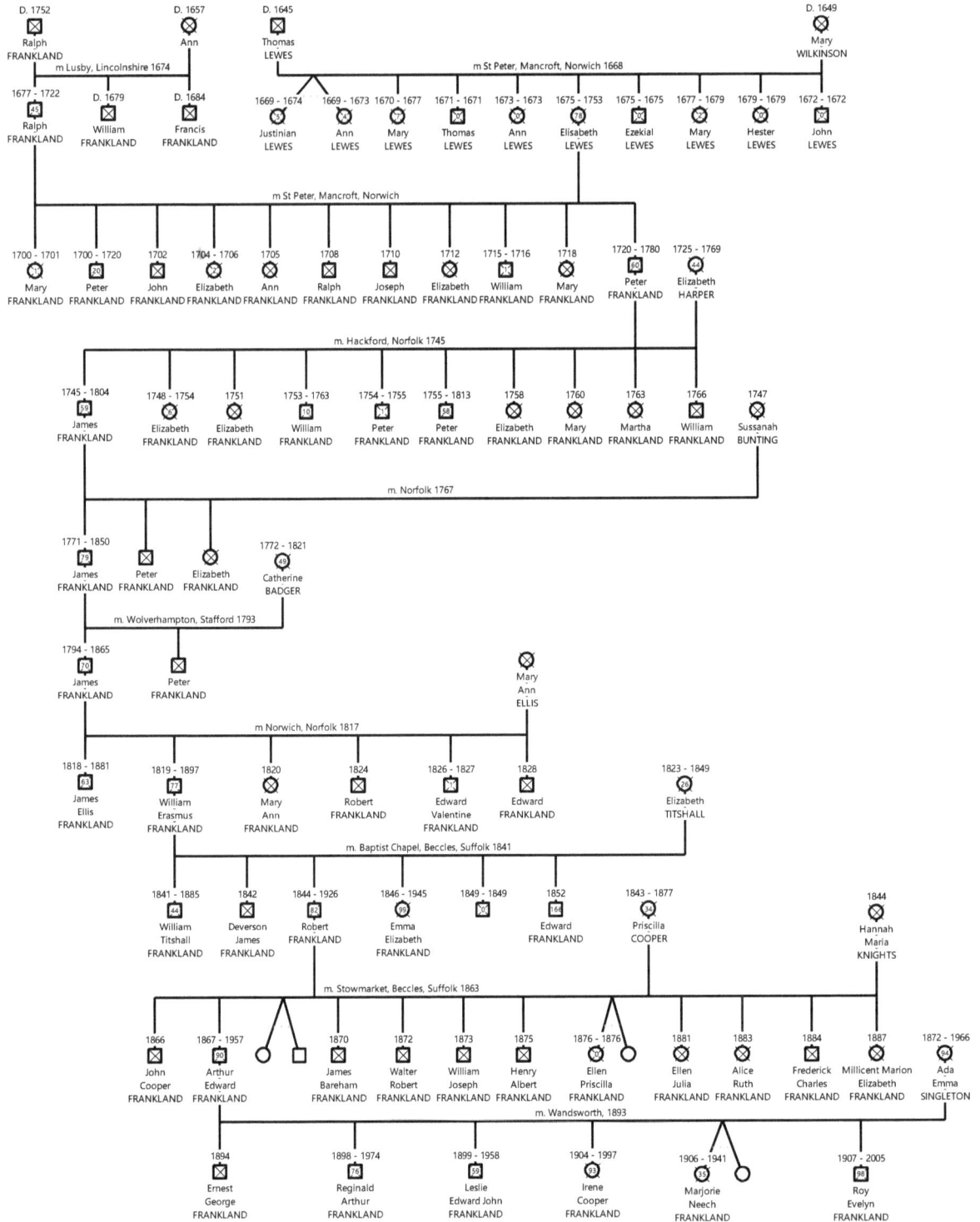

Genealogical chart of the Frankland family.

Top generation:
- D. 1752 — Ralph FRANKLAND
- D. 1657 — Ann
- D. 1645 — Thomas LEWES
- D. 1649 — Mary WILKINSON

m Lusby, Lincolnshire 1674 · m St Peter, Mancroft, Norwich 1668

- 1677 - 1722 Ralph FRANKLAND (43)
- D. 1679 William FRANKLAND
- D. 1684 Francis FRANKLAND
- 1669 - 1674 Justinian LEWES
- 1669 - 1673 Ann LEWES
- 1670 - 1677 Mary LEWES
- 1671 - 1671 Thomas LEWES
- 1673 - 1673 Ann LEWES
- 1675 - 1753 Elisabeth LEWES
- 1675 - 1675 Ezekial LEWES
- 1677 - 1679 Mary LEWES
- 1679 - 1679 Hester LEWES
- 1672 - 1672 John LEWES

m St Peter, Mancroft, Norwich

- 1700 - 1701 Mary FRANKLAND
- 1700 - 1720 Peter FRANKLAND (20)
- 1702 John FRANKLAND
- 1704 - 1706 Elizabeth FRANKLAND
- 1705 Ann FRANKLAND
- 1708 Ralph FRANKLAND
- 1710 Joseph FRANKLAND
- 1712 Elizabeth FRANKLAND
- 1715 - 1716 William FRANKLAND
- 1718 Mary FRANKLAND
- 1720 - 1780 Peter FRANKLAND (60)
- 1725 - 1769 Elizabeth HARPER (44)

m. Hackford, Norfolk 1745

- 1745 - 1804 James FRANKLAND (59)
- 1748 - 1754 Elizabeth FRANKLAND
- 1751 Elizabeth FRANKLAND
- 1753 - 1763 William FRANKLAND (10)
- 1754 - 1755 Peter FRANKLAND
- 1755 - 1813 Peter FRANKLAND (58)
- 1758 Elizabeth FRANKLAND
- 1760 Mary FRANKLAND
- 1763 Martha FRANKLAND
- 1766 William FRANKLAND
- 1747 Sussanah BUNTING

m. Norfolk 1767

- 1771 - 1850 James FRANKLAND (79)
- Peter FRANKLAND
- Elizabeth FRANKLAND
- 1772 - 1821 Catherine BADGER (49)

m. Wolverhampton, Stafford 1793

- 1794 - 1865 James FRANKLAND (70)
- Peter FRANKLAND
- Mary Ann ELLIS

m Norwich, Norfolk 1817

- 1818 - 1881 James Ellis FRANKLAND (63)
- 1819 - 1897 William Erasmus FRANKLAND (77)
- 1820 Mary Ann FRANKLAND
- 1824 Robert FRANKLAND
- 1826 - 1827 Edward Valentine FRANKLAND
- 1828 Edward FRANKLAND
- 1823 - 1849 Elizabeth TITSHALL (26)

m. Baptist Chapel, Beccles, Suffolk 1841

- 1841 - 1885 William Titshall FRANKLAND (44)
- 1842 Deverson James FRANKLAND
- 1844 - 1926 Robert FRANKLAND (82)
- 1846 - 1945 Emma Elizabeth FRANKLAND (99)
- 1849 - 1849
- 1852 Edward FRANKLAND
- 1843 - 1877 Priscilla COOPER (33)
- 1844 Hannah Maria KNIGHTS

m. Stowmarket, Beccles, Suffolk 1863

- 1866 John Cooper FRANKLAND
- 1867 - 1957 Arthur Edward FRANKLAND (90)
- 1870 James Bareham FRANKLAND
- 1872 Walter Robert FRANKLAND
- 1873 William Joseph FRANKLAND
- 1875 Henry Albert FRANKLAND
- 1876 - 1876 Ellen Priscilla FRANKLAND
- 1881 Ellen Julia FRANKLAND
- 1883 Alice Ruth FRANKLAND
- 1884 Frederick Charles FRANKLAND
- 1887 Millicent Marion Elizabeth FRANKLAND
- 1872 - 1966 Ada Emma SINGLETON (94)

m. Wandsworth, 1893

- 1894 Ernest George FRANKLAND
- 1898 - 1974 Reginald Arthur FRANKLAND (76)
- 1899 - 1958 Leslie Edward John FRANKLAND (59)
- 1904 - 1997 Irene Cooper FRANKLAND (93)
- 1906 - 1941 Marjorie Neech FRANKLAND (35)
- 1907 - 2005 Roy Evelyn FRANKLAND (98)

The name Frankland first appears in Yorkshire, where they held a family seat from 1587 and were Lords of the manor of Thirkelby in Auldwark (Aldwark), Yorkshire. The Manor was passed from father to son and in one case, uncle to nephew, along with the title Baronet. It was interesting to find that the second Baronet, Sir Thomas Frankland was married to Elizabeth Russell. Elizabeth was the daughter of Sir John Russell, forth Baronet of Chippenham, and his wife Frances Cromwell, daughter of Oliver!

The death, in 1849, of Sir Robert Frankland, saw the Manor pass to his daughter Augusta Louisa who had married Thomas, fifth Lord Walsingham. Her son Thomas, Lord Walsingham then became Lord of the Manor.

The visitations of Norfolk show two Franklands and their wives: Sir Henry Frankland and his wife Frances and Thomas Frankland with his wife Bridget. Both Henry and Thomas are 'of Auldwark, York'. It was in the area of Aylsham, north Norfolk, that they settled, and this is where we find the connections to our own family. With my 7xG Grandfather Peter Frankland marrying Elizabeth Harper, in 1745, in Hackford, Aylsham.

The first Frankland recorded in Suffolk was William Erasmus Frankland (known by his middle name, Erasmus, later in life). Erasmus was Peter and Elizabeth's Great Great Grandson. He was a harness maker and saddler, the hereditary occupation of this branch of the Frankland family and son of James Frankland and Mary Ann Ellis. William settled in Beccles, where he married Elizabeth Titshall and, initially, lived with her parents. Between 1841 and 1849 the couple had five children: William, Deverson (known by his middle name James), Robert and Emma, as well as a baby who died shortly after birth. Around that time William's brother Robert and sister Mary Ann followed him to Beccles, and by the time of the 1851 Census, William and his second wife Charlotte, with three of his children were living in the same house as Robert and Mary Ann. Subsequently, Charlotte also had a son, Edward.

The brothers set up in business together making saddles, harnesses and grease, a thriving business of the time.

William's first son William also became a harness maker, but after staying with his uncle James Ellis Frankland's family, in London, decided to settle there with his wife Maria and, subsequently, three children. His second son James, married Esther Neech and became a master baker in Beccles before moving to Battersea in the mid 1870s. He had become a Primitive Methodist speaker in 1869, and continued to fulfil this calling in Battersea, as leader at the Grayshot Road Church, part of the Lavender Hill Circuit. Over time, he took a number of jobs in Battersea including wine-cellarman, labourer and French polisher.

William's third son Robert, another harness maker, remained in Beccles taking his place in the family business alongside his father. In time, Robert's own son John would also become a harness maker and join the business. By 1871, Edward, William's youngest son was a coach trimmer, probably also associated with the saddle and harness business. By that time, however, William had died.

After first courting Rebecca Neech, who lived in Fenn lane, close to the Frankland's saddlery business, Robert had met Priscilla Cooper. They married in Beccles, in 1863. Sadly, Priscilla died aged 34, leaving Robert and their six boys, (they had already lost their four baby daughters, two sets of twins). Robert remained in Beccles living in New Market Place and two years after Priscilla's death he remarried. His new wife was Hannah Maria Knights, niece of his father-in-law, John Cooper's second wife Anne. Robert and Hannah had a further three daughters and one son.

Over time, Robert and Priscilla's sons all left Beccles. Their uncles, William and James, had already moved to London. It is in looking at this migration from Beccles to Battersea that it is possible to see the kindness and family support offered by our ancestors towards each other.

Their eldest son, John Cooper Frankland, left Beccles aged about thirty years and moved in with his brother Arthur and sister-in-law Ada. He was with them in 1901 at 115, Eversleigh Road, as a boarder. He remained with them through their move to 205, still unmarried in 1911, and continuing to follow his trade, as a harness maker.

Arthur Edward Frankland, had himself moved to London with his brother James Bareham Frankland. They initially, stayed with their Uncle James (Deverson) Frankland and his wife Esther (nee Neech) at 152, Eversleigh Road. By 1901, James B had become a greengrocer and was living in Lavender Hill, while Arthur had moved up the road, to 115, with his wife.

Walter Robert Frankland was younger, still in his teens, when he moved from Beccles to Battersea. He was, by 1891, living with John Singleton and his wife Rebecca (nee Neech), at 205, Eversleigh Road. He was working as an ironmonger's assistant. Also staying at the house, was Rebecca's younger sister Susanna (another migrant from Beccles) and their four children. Walter continued to live at 205, and in 1901, he was there with John, now a widower, and one of John's daughters. Ten years on, in 1911, he was living at 51, Eversleigh Road, with his wife Susanna and daughter Eva. Walter was then an ironmonger's storekeeper.

Henry Frankland

William Joseph Frankland, although choosing not to move to London, was living in Portsmouth, with his Irish wife, Ruth, in 1901. His brother Henry Albert Frankland, the youngest of Robert and Priscilla's children, moved the shortest distance from Beccles. He set up home with his wife Edith, in Ipswich and continued to work as a harness maker.

So, Arthur Frankland, Robert's second eldest son, married Ada Singleton, in 1893 and they set up home, at number 115, Eversleigh Road. Arthur was a railway clerk and it seems likely that 115 had been a rental property, so the opportunity of living at 205, Ada's childhood home would have been very welcome. Ada's mother and father, Rebecca and John Singleton, had moved to live with Arthur's aunt, Emma Riddington (nee Frankland). At this time, they would have already had four children. By 1911, the house must have felt quite crowded with Ada and Arthur, six children and John Frankland, Arthur's older brother living there.

Three Generations of the Frankland Family
Left to right: Robert, Ernest and Arthur

Back row left to right:

Leslie Edward John
Frankland
Ernest George Frankland
Arthur Edward Frankland
Uncle John Frankland

Middle row left to right:

Irene Cooper Frankland
Hannah Amy Frankland
(nee Richardson)
Roy Evelyn Frankland
Ada Emma Frankland
-

Front row left to right:

Marjorie Neech Frankland
-

Ernest, the eldest son, worked at Somerset House, in London. He married Hannah Amy Richardson (Amy), in 1919. Unfortunately, though desperate for children, Amy miscarried easily and it wasn't until ten years after their marriage that Ernest and Amy had a daughter, Sylvia.

Amy suffered post-natal depression and throughout Sylvia's early childhood, she continued to be greatly affected by mental health issues. Amy had expressed anxiety that she might harm her husband or precious daughter and instead, tragically, she took her own life.

Ernest and his ten-year-old daughter moved in with his sister Irene and her husband Stanley Parfitt. This was a larger house in Cheam. Later, when Irene and Stanley moved, with their young son Graeme, Ada, Arthur and Ernest's youngest sister Marjorie joined Sylvia and her father. Thus it was that Sylvia became particularly close to her grandparents.

Sylvia with Grandfather Arthur on her wedding day

Ernest was an intelligent man, who was reported to do the work of three men. Languages, were his interest; he could speak several and read more. His death was sudden and unexpected. Suffering from influenza, he collapsed, striking his head on the fireplace. Ernest died of a cerebral haemorrhage. He was 51.

Reginald Arthur Frankland

Reginald, Ada and Arthur's second son, married Winifred North in 1921. A year later, they had a son and then twin boys.

Reg with wife Winnie

Reginald and Winifred's sons

Leslie Edward John Frankland

Leslie (my grandfather) was a kind man, who was never known to say anything bad about anyone. He showed talents in technical drawing and draughtsmanship and had wished to pursue a career in that field, however, wartime needs channelled his choices and he became a railway engineer, curvature of the spine preventing him from enlisting in the armed services.

Mildred Smith (Milly)

Leslie married nineteen-year-old Mildred Smith (Milly), in 1925. She was working as a dressmaker at the time.

Milly was thrilled to find that she was expecting a child in the first year of their marriage, but the baby boy was very large and died during labour, subsequently having to be extracted surgically. This must have been devastating for the young couple.

Jean Frankland

Milly continued as a dressmaker, being a very skilled needlewoman. Then in 1928, she gave birth to Jean, a beautiful dark-haired girl. Jean was petite and as a child loved to dance.

Sadly, tragedy was to befall Leslie and Milly again two years later, when they were expecting twins. One of the twins died in utero and two weeks later Milly lost both, a girl and a boy, while fighting septicaemia. Later, my mother Elaine was born followed by Leslie and Milly's youngest child, Diana.

Left to right - Diana and Elaine Frankland

It was around this time that Ada and Arthur gave them the opportunity to move in to 205, Eversleigh Road, which was gratefully taken up.

Irene Cooper Frankland

Rene, Stanley and one of their sons

Rene and Stanley's sons

Irene (Rene) married Stanley Parfitt in 1931 and had two sons.

Rene, loved to keep in touch with family and was a great letter-writer, often sending old photos and words of praise and encouragement. The family lived in Vicarage Lane, Marlborough for many years. It was there that Bill and I met them for the first time, although I had been corresponding with Rene for a number of years.

Marjorie Neech Frankland

Marjorie was the youngest daughter of Ada and Arthur, the only survivor of twin girls. She was unwell for much of her life, a favourite aunt of her niece Sylvia.

The youngest of the family was Roy. Roy married Lilian (Lily) Brown in 1934. They had two children, a son and daughter.

Roy Evelyn Frankland

Lily and Roy Frankland

Lily and Roy's son and daughter

The following was written by Sylvia about her aunt Marjorie:

'One of the most significant figures of my childhood was my father's younger sister, my Aunt Marjorie. I think there was always a particular bond between us because for the first two years of my life, my mother and father and I lived with his parents in the crowded little family home, 205, Eversleigh Road, Battersea. Living there, as well as my grandparents and Marjorie, were my aunt Irene and my uncle Roy, both still unmarried. How seven adults and a very vocal baby managed to live together amicably in these circumstances is a tribute to the tolerance of all concerned.

My mother was suffering from post-natal depression and so the care of me fell largely on Grandma and Marjorie, who was then twenty, but did not work because of poor health. A baby in the household was no doubt a great interest, and Grandma, then in her fifties, with experience of bringing up a large family, had a calm competence in dealing with day to day upheavals.

Marjorie was born in February 1906, and was named Marjorie Neech Frankland, Neech being the maiden surname of her maternal grandmother. As the survivor of twins, she was always very small and slight, never quite growing to five feet in height. But she made up for her small stature with plenty of spirit and was a lively girl, full of fun. She always regretted the loss of her twin and adopted as a substitute her elder sister Irene. They remained devoted all their lives. In fact, when Irene went to school Marjorie was so unhappy that she was allowed to go too, a tiny three-year-old who followed the teacher round, holding on to her skirt. Later, she and Irene, in company with several girl cousins, attended the High School in Broomwood Road, Clapham. She was ambidextrous and had a very active mind, interested in many things, but she was not academic, and attempts by Ernest, her studious elder brother (my father), to teach her and her sister extra French, usually found her reading fairy stories instead.

As a girl, she was liable to go off into fits of giggles, especially at meal times, in which Irene and Roy would join, to Grandpa's annoyance. When she was a teenager, she could occasionally make crashingly tactless remarks, though with no malicious intent. She was not pretty, but nice looking, with very thick dark brown hair and large grey-blue eyes. In summer, her face was usually covered with freckles.

She left school at sixteen and got a clerical job in the City. It was around this time that she developed rheumatic fever. Sadly, her heart was affected and she never went out to work again.

When I first remember her, she was still reasonably well, though inclined to tire easily. But she was never too tired to play games of make-believe, like flying off on a magic carpet to distant lands. All children loved her and she was great fun at parties. She encouraged me in many activities and when I was ill she wrote me lovely letters, enclosing pictures and cut-outs to amuse me. Once, when my cousins Eric and Douglas and I were all staying at 205, she taught us to read. I can recall all three of us sitting in a row on the kitchen table. We must have been almost six. She would have made a good infant teacher, for although always kind and amusing, she was not over indulgent and could be quite firm. Years later, when I started to learn Latin at school, she learnt some too, and at one stage was further advanced in the text book than me. And in spite of a juvenile preference for fairy stories her French was good enough to read postcards from my father in French when he and my mother were on holiday in Belgium or Brittany. She sewed, knitted and embroidered neatly and well; I can remember her making a little white-lined coat for Murray, and when Graeme was born she knitted a most beautiful lacy shawl. I still have it today, very fragile now, having used it for my own children.

I think it must have been about this time that she took lessons in hairdressing, and a number of regular customers, in whom she took great interest, came to have their hair shampooed and set in the front room at 205. Grandma would carry buckets of hot water to and fro and it was probably all rather 'Heath Robinson'. But it kept her in touch with the outside world and earned her some pocket money to make her feel independent.

Hairdressing was a very different matter in those days. The hair was normally set in rigid, unnatural waves, achieved in two possible ways. They could be formed with curling tongs, an old method and one that had to be done carefully. The tongs were heated on a gas ring and must not get too hot or they would burn the hair off in lumps instead of curling it. Alternatively, the wet hair was set in a 'water wave', by hand, after a liberal application of setting lotion, a thick, sticky fluid. Waves were pressed into place and fixed with metal clips, and the hair ends were twisted into tight curls also fixed by little clips. The victim was then placed under the hood of a large standing drier and the hair blown dry by an electric current, a kind of baking process which lasted about half an hour and could become painfully hot. Hair could also be subjected to fearsomely strong permanent waving, but I don't think Marjorie was equipped to do this.

I suppose I was about four or five when I spent a summer holiday with my parents at Mundesley on the Norfolk coast, staying in a guest house opposite the old windmill there. An extended Scottish family called Smith were staying there as well, and as there were several children we all became friendly. Marjorie came down to spend part of the time with us, and this was how she met Murray Smith, an adult son of the family. He was tall and good-looking, and they were clearly attracted to each other. After the holiday was over they corresponded in the rather formal and stilted way of those days. His letters survive, she kept them all.

At this juncture she had another set-back. Because she had always suffered for throat infections, her doctor decided that she should have her tonsils out, apparently not taking her heart condition into account. An operation from which most people recovered in a few days, kept her in hospital quite ill for six weeks and her health was further badly affected. From this time, she never walked upstairs – once down in the morning she was down for the day, and Grandpa carried her up to bed at night. She was a very light weight: when I was a hefty twelve-year-old I could carry her quite easily.

Murray Smith then wrote asking to visit her, as he was coming to London on business (I think he was an accountant), and she had the courage to reply, telling him of her deterioration in health and asking him not to come. She knew that she would never be in a fit state to contemplate marriage, but the cost of the decision must have been great. She never spoke of it, giving some spurious excuse when I asked her if he was coming. Only in occasional unguarded moment did she ever give way to her weakness and the limitations it imposed. She was an extrovert and adventurous person, who would have loved to travel and see the world, but everything seemed taken from her. But she remained grateful for the love and care of her parents and family and was always affectionate and interested in the doings of those around her.

It was during the 30s that she changed her doctor and came under Dr Max Sayers. He prescribed Digitalis for her, which slowed down her over-active heart, and for some time seemed to help. Then came the move from 205, Eversleigh Road to 42, Holland Avenue in the summer of 1939.

My mother had died in 1936 and for over two years, my father and I lived with my aunt Irene and her husband Stanley Parfitt. They had generously made room for us in their house in north Cheam and we subsequently all moved to a larger house in Holland Avenue, Cheam. But they then decided to move again, with their little three-year-old son Graeme, to a nearby bungalow, and my father asked, with some trepidation, whether Grandma and Grandpa and auntie Marjorie would like to come and live with us. He feared that their long associations in Clapham and Battersea would hold them back, but to our delight they were over-joyed, and the changeover took place only weeks before the war broke out.

This meant another change of doctor. Dr Phillips did not believe in strong drugs and took Marjorie off Digitalis suddenly and completely, substituting other medication which was never very effective. This was really the beginning of the end for her, and the last two years of her life were a catalogue of increasing ailments, patiently borne.

Just after the move to Cheam, my uncle and aunt, Roy and Lily, had a son, born on July 5th 1939, whom they named Murray after the man Marjorie might have married. I don't know whether she knew in advance that they intended to do this, but I can recall the first time she saw the baby – she was getting over a brief illness and held him in her arms while sitting up in bed. A longer visit was at Christmas 1939, a happy time, when they stayed with us for several days.

The next years were ones of constant change with people coming and going, especially those closest to her. Stanley, Irene and Graeme departed for rural Wiltshire, where uncle worked as a local draughtsman in an aircraft factory; and in September 1940, my father, a civil servant in the Inland Revenue, was evacuated to North Wales. I followed him a few weeks later. Other members of the family stayed for varying periods to escape the bombing in London or when bombed out. Marjorie's letters to my father and me were lively and newsy, with amusing anecdotes about the War, but she was becoming increasingly weary of all the hustle and bustle and could not always hide this. She was more and more often ill with a variety of ailments and was diagnosed as having angina. It was this which killed her, with a sudden fatal attack one hot June day in 1941. She was 35.

She was not afraid to die; several years before she had described death to me as nothing more than opening a door and passing into another room, and when it came she welcomed it as an escape from suffering, saying to Grandma, who had nursed her so devotedly through numerous illnesses, 'Mother, let me go'. A few days before, she had told Grandpa with great sincerity what wonderful parents they had been to her.

One tends to take familiar people for granted, especially when young. Although I knew she was not as strong as other people, it never seemed necessary to treat her differently from anyone else, just as it seemed a matter of course, if I was sleeping with her on a visit, to find her sitting up in bed in the middle of the night, fighting for breath. She hardly ever complained. It is only with hindsight that one realises what courage and strength of character she had, and what a deep faith, of which she rarely spoke. Her life could so easily have been a tragedy, instead it became a triumph.'

So, 205, Eversleigh Road saw a great deal of our family. Milly and Leslie saw their three daughters grow up at the house, attending school locally.

During the war years, everyone was reliant on rations and queuing for precious commodities became a part of daily life. Elaine was aware that, when there was not enough food to go around, Milly would feed the family, saying she would have her meal later. Of course, she would really go without.

Elaine recounted that Leslie was in the Home Guard and had to wear a 'great coat'. Being a slight man, the coat fell to his ankles!

As a child, she remembers being evacuated to Brighton for a time. The property being at the back of a dairy. The majority of the war years though, were spent in Battersea. Bombing raids, became commonplace, but she always resisted going to the shelters, afraid of being trapped. The choice, instead was to go to the underground station and down onto the platform, or remain at home, both of which she preferred. Towards the end of the war, it was the 'silent bombs' that were the most frightening, for their lack of any warning of proximity. Thankfully, the family were all there to celebrate when peace was finally declared, in 1945.

Having no sons, it was Elaine who was taken by her father to Chelsea football matches. She became quite a fan and loved the time spent with her father, who she adored.

Milly and Leslie's eldest daughter Jean, who I remember as lively and spirited, open and caring, married Jim Oram, a gentle, devoted and sincere man. They had three daughters and one son.

Elaine worked for a time as a comptometer operator. This was perhaps a precursor to the computer and suited her quick mathematical skills. At 19, she married Albert Willis and settled in Morden, Surrey. My older sister and I were both born at 205 Eversleigh Road, it being commonplace in the 1950s for a daughter to be with her mother for the birth of her babies, husbands still being encouraged to stay away. My younger sister, though, was born at home, in Morden. Being a third child, there was little time to fetch the midwife, no time at all to travel across town to her mother's house!

It was towards the end of the 1950s, that Leslie became ill. He had arranged to meet Elaine, Bert and girls at Victoria station, following a summer holiday. He drove them home, but left straight away, saying that he was very tired. A short time later, Leslie phoned them. He explained where he was, and that he needed help. Bert ran all the way, a considerable distance, having no car at that time, and found Leslie slumped in the phone box.

Leslie Frankland

Leslie managed to explain that as he was driving, his hand kept falling from the steering wheel. He had suffered a stroke.

Leslie was unable to return home for around five months and only then because Milly insisted he be released to her care. Showing huge determination, he learned to walk again and to write with his right hand (being naturally left-handed). Day by day he was pleased to show off his newly acquired skills. He was also able to appreciate how highly he was regarded by others, from the constant stream of visitors to the house. Youngest daughter Diana, still living at home at the time, amazed her father by offering to decorate the lounge (a job that had been next on the list of 'to dos' and for which the wallpaper and paint had already been purchased). She did an excellent job, discovering another range of hidden talents. Sadly, around three months from his return home, Leslie suffered a second devastating stroke and died, aged 58 years.

Milly remained at '205' for a while with her youngest daughter Diana. The house was finally sold when the two decided to try to set up a boarding house to procure a much-needed income. Having once been a dressmaker, Milly continued to enjoy sewing and knitting until rheumatoid arthritis robbed her of the dexterity required to carry out the fine, detailed work. It must have made her proud though, to witness the same skills, passed on to daughters Elaine and Diana, both able to turn their hands to the most intricate of tasks. Milly continued to live with Diana after her marriage to Roger Wiles, an active, engaging and sociable man. Roger would often joke with Milly, 'pulling her leg' and sending her into fits of laughter, or more often triggering a look of pretend outrage. Despite increasing disability, her wit and enthusiasm for all things 'family' were constant.

Mildred (Milly) Frankland (nee Smith)

Elaine's love of sewing and knitting meant that as we were growing up, there was always something 'in production', usually for one of us. Today, she is more often tackling the finest embroidery or knitting for the youngest generation of her treasured and now quite extensive family.

Ada (nee Singleton) and Arthur Frankland

Sylvia and George Colman

Stan and Rene Parfitt with Lily and Roy Frankland

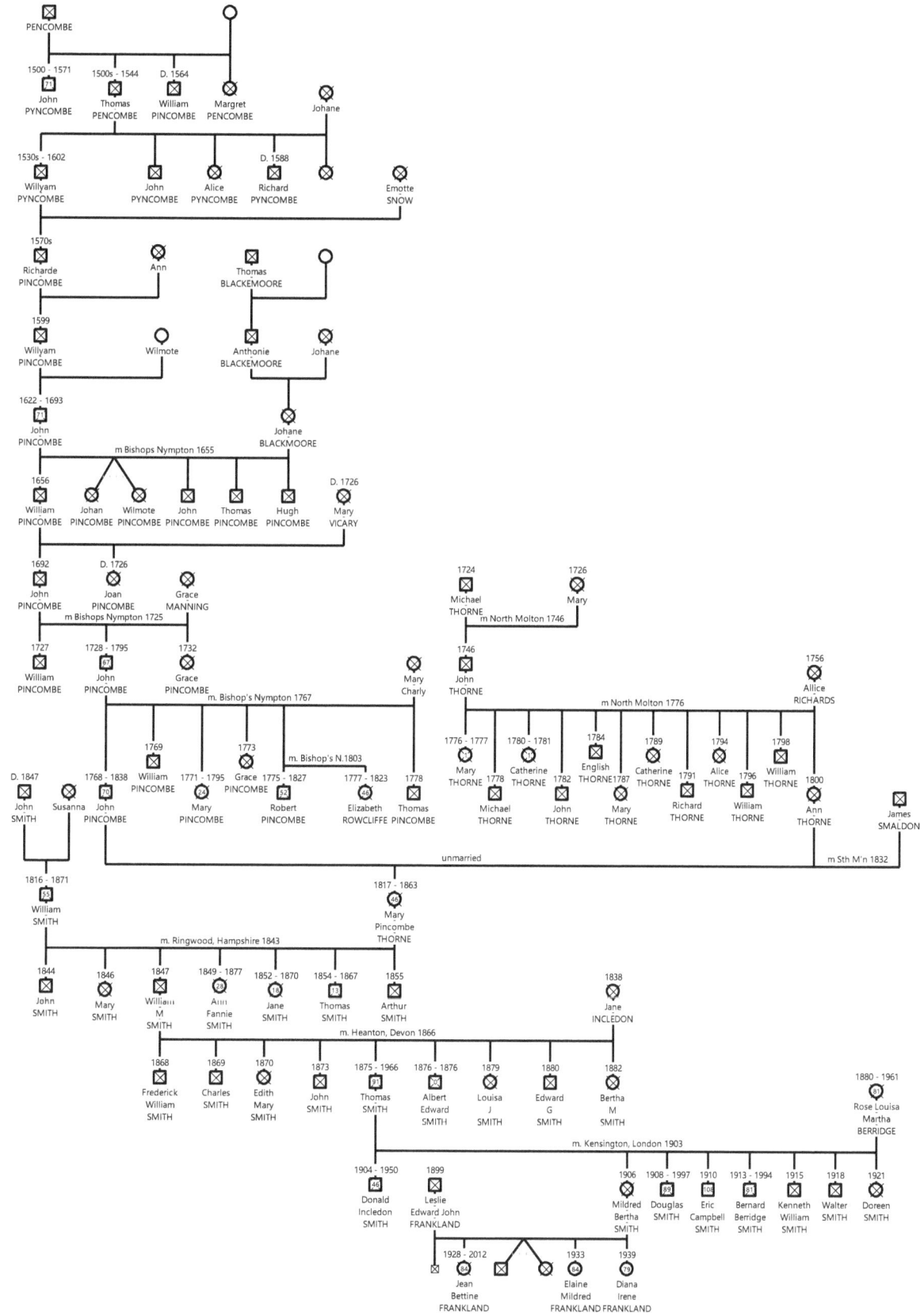

The Smiths

PENCOMBE

1500 - 1571
John PYNCOMBE [71]

1500s - 1544
Thomas PENCOMBE

D. 1564
William PINCOMBE

Margret PENCOMBE

Johane

1530s - 1602
Willyam PYNCOMBE

John PYNCOMBE

Alice PYNCOMBE

D. 1588
Richard PYNCOMBE

Emotte SNOW

1570s
Richarde PINCOMBE

Ann

Thomas BLACKEMOORE

1599
Willyam PINCOMBE

Wilmote

Anthonie BLACKEMOORE

Johane

1622 - 1693
John PINCOMBE [71]

Johane BLACKMOORE

m Bishops Nympton 1655

1656
William PINCOMBE

Johan PINCOMBE

Wilmote PINCOMBE

John PINCOMBE

Thomas PINCOMBE

Hugh PINCOMBE

D. 1726
Mary VICARY

1692
John PINCOMBE

D. 1726
Joan PINCOMBE

Grace MANNING

m Bishops Nympton 1725

1727
William PINCOMBE

1728 - 1795
John PINCOMBE [67]

1732
Grace PINCOMBE

Mary Charly

1724
Michael THORNE

1726
Mary

m North Molton 1746

1746
John THORNE

m. Bishop's Nympton 1767

1769
William PINCOMBE

1771 - 1795
Mary PINCOMBE

1773
Grace PINCOMBE

m. Bishop's N.1803

1775 - 1827
Robert PINCOMBE

1777 - 1823
Elizabeth ROWCLIFFE

1778
Thomas PINCOMBE

m North Molton 1776

1776 - 1777
Mary THORNE

1778
Michael THORNE

1780 - 1781
Catherine THORNE

1782
John THORNE

1784
English THORNE 1787

1789
Catherine THORNE

1791
Mary THORNE

1794
Alice THORNE

1796
William THORNE

1798
William THORNE

1800
Ann THORNE

1756
Allice RICHARDS

James SMALDON

D. 1847
John SMITH

Susanna

1768 - 1838
John PINCOMBE [70]

1816 - 1871
William SMITH [53]

unmarried

m Sth M'n 1832

1817 - 1863
Mary Pincombe THORNE [46]

m. Ringwood, Hampshire 1843

1844
John SMITH

1846
Mary SMITH

1847
William M SMITH

1849 - 1877
Ann Fannie SMITH

1852 - 1870
Jane SMITH

1854 - 1867
Thomas SMITH

1855
Arthur SMITH

1838
Jane INCLEDON

m. Heanton, Devon 1866

1868
Frederick William SMITH

1869
Charles SMITH

1870
Edith Mary SMITH

1873
John SMITH

1875 - 1966
Thomas SMITH

1876 - 1876
Albert Edward SMITH

1879
Louisa J SMITH

1880
Edward G SMITH

1882
Bertha M SMITH

1880 - 1961
Rose Louisa Martha BERRIDGE

m. Kensington, London 1903

1904 - 1950
Donald Incledon SMITH [46]

1899
Leslie Edward John FRANKLAND

1906
Mildred Bertha SMITH

1908 - 1997
Douglas SMITH [89]

1910
Eric Campbell SMITH

1913 - 1994
Bernard Berridge SMITH [81]

1915
Kenneth William SMITH

1918
Walter SMITH

1921
Doreen SMITH

1928 - 2012
Jean Bettine FRANKLAND

1933
Elaine Mildred FRANKLAND

1939
Diana Irene FRANKLAND

As the reader might expect, Smith has not been the easiest of names to research. The earliest Smith that I can be sure of was John, born between 1781-5, died 1847. John was an excise officer and married to Susanna. Their son, William, was born in Litton Cheney in Dorset, in 1816. John and Susanna were living in Ringwood, Hampshire in 1841, and from the Census it is possible to see that they were not born in the area. William was married to Mary Pincombe Thorne at the Parish Church of St Peter and St Paul in Ringwood, in 1843. The marriage certificate tells us that William had followed his father in becoming an excise officer. John Pincombe, farmer, is named as Mary's father, but interestingly, the name and profession have been crossed out. Over the top is written in Latin 'Nullius Filia'.

Mary Pincombe Thorne was born in 1817. Her Christening was recorded in Molland, Devon, 1819. Only her mother was named, Ann Thorne. Ann herself, was the youngest child of John Thorne and Allice (nee Richards) who had thirteen children. She was born in 1800, so was only seventeen when Mary was born. Mary's marriage certificate had already alluded to who her father was, but finding his Will, confirmed her parentage. John's will states:

> 'I give and devise and bequeath unto my natural Daughter Mary Pincombe Thorne, Daughter of Ann Smaldon all that freehold Estate called Great Woods in the parish of Molland with the appurtenances situate lying and being in the aforesaid parish Molland unto her and unto her Children lawfully begotten and unto her heirs for ever. My will is that my said Daughter Mary Pincombe Thorne shall have the whole of the freehold property left by me at my decease on her attaining the age of twenty-one years....
>
> ....I also give and bequeath unto Mary Pincombe Thorne my Copyhold Estate called Lower Eastweek situated in the parish of Bishopsnympton when she attains the age of Twenty four years. All the rest residue and remainder of my property wheresoever and whatsoever I give upon trust unto Thomas Pincombe my Brother and William Pincombe Jun[io]r of Bishopsnympton whom I nominate and appoint sole Executors of this my last Will and Testament the[y] are to pay and receive all monies connected with the property real and personal by me at my decease until my Daughter Mary Pincombe Thorne shall attain the age of twenty four years when she is to have the whole of such property in the hands of my Executors in trust. My Will is that my Executors in trust are to pay unto Mary Pincombe Thorne the sum Forty pounds a year to be paid in two half yearly paym[en]ts.'

And so, to the Pincombes:

The first, named Pencombe, to be recorded in Devon, arrived with Lord de la Zouche in 1485 following the Battle of Bosworth Field, where they supported Richard III. There is speculation, that this family was located at Pencombe Manor, Herefordshire and fled to the Devon area in order to escape the effects of having supported Richard III against King Henry VII who won the Battle of Bosworth Field, in 1485. There were four children from this Pencombe:

John Pyncombe, born about 1500 and died in South Molton, Devon in 1571. John married the daughter of Richard Dodridge and had two sons, John and Christopher.

Thomas Pencombe, who died in 1544, in North Molton. Thomas married Johane and had five children: William, John, Alice, Richard and one further daughter.

William Pincombe, who was buried in North Molton in 1564. William married Elizabeth and had two daughters, Agnes and Mary.

Margret Pencombe, who married Phillip Kingdon. They had two daughters, Johane and Emote.

It is Thomas and Johane that are my 12xG Grandparents.

It appears that one branch of the Pincombe Family at South Molton was entitled to bear the family coat of arms. The Royal College granted this to John Pyncombe (elder brother of our Thomas) in 1616. John was married to Amy Dodridge (daughter of Richard Dodridge of Barnstaple). His son John, Barrister of the Middle Temple, also bore these arms. He was married to Mary, daughter of Sir John Carew of Crowcombe. It is not clear whether John's son Richard Pincombe ever bore these arms. It was only a year from John's death to that of Richard. Richard's sister Gertrude, however, may have borne these arms as the eldest daughter, but it would have ended with her. The Pyncombe Trust, which still exists today, was formed with the wealth of this branch of the Pincombe family.

Generations of Pincombes lived in the North and South Molton areas of Devon. It was here that they owned and farmed land. Mary Pincombe Thorne's father John, had been the main inheritor of his father's Will, being the first born. John resided at Great Woods, in Molland, North Molton. This is now a listed building with outbuildings and farmland. He also owned as 'copyhold' (similar to lease hold) a property called East Week, in Bishop's Nympton, another farm. It is not clear how Ann Thorne came to know John, but her father was also a local farmer. John was significantly older than Ann. He was 49 when Mary was born, whilst Ann was only 17. Neither had any further children. John never married, but Ann married James Smalden, at the age of 32.

It appears that Mary's birth was not covered up, as might have happened at that time, given the apparent circumstances. She knew her father and his family from the beginning of her life.

John died in 1838, following a demise in health, during which time he had updated his Will. He told Mary that he had made provision for her after his death. Mary was living at Great Woods at the time of John's death, and the Will reading at the house followed his funeral. Although there were some disgruntled nephews, it appears that the Will was accepted and taken away by John's brothers, William and Thomas, as his executers. The Will was proved and payments made to those inheriting lesser amounts. Mary was given twenty pounds (half the yearly allowance, presumably to last six months), but as a minor, she would need to wait for the transfer of property and her financial inheritance. John was buried at St Mary's Church in Molland. His grave reads,

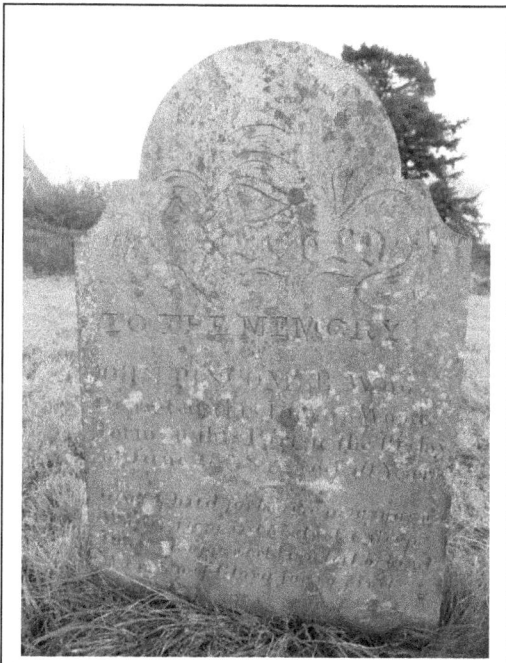

To the memory of John Pincombe

Who departed this life at Woods Farm

in this Parish the 19th day of June 1838

Aged 70 Years

Mary turned twenty-one shortly after John's death and then turned twenty-four in 1841, but despite seeking settlement from Thomas (as William had by that time died) her requests were ignored. At that time, she was living with her mother and step-father, in South Molton, whilst tenant farmers resided at Great Woods and East Week.

Mary married William Smith in Ringwood, Hampshire, his parents' home, in 1843. As an excise officer, it is likely that William was well aware of legal and financial matters. Pending settlement, the couple set up home in Williton, Somerset, near the Devon boarder. Letters were sent from the Smiths' solicitor to Thomas Pincombe, but they remained unanswered. Finally, the only avenue seemed to be court action.

Bill and I went to the National Archives in London and were able to see the original records of the court action. Written in small copper plate script on large, approximately A1 sized, sheets of parchment, the records were difficult and extremely time-consuming to digest, there being around fifty pages in all!

National Archives London

The lines are so long, paper markers are needed to track from one side to the other.

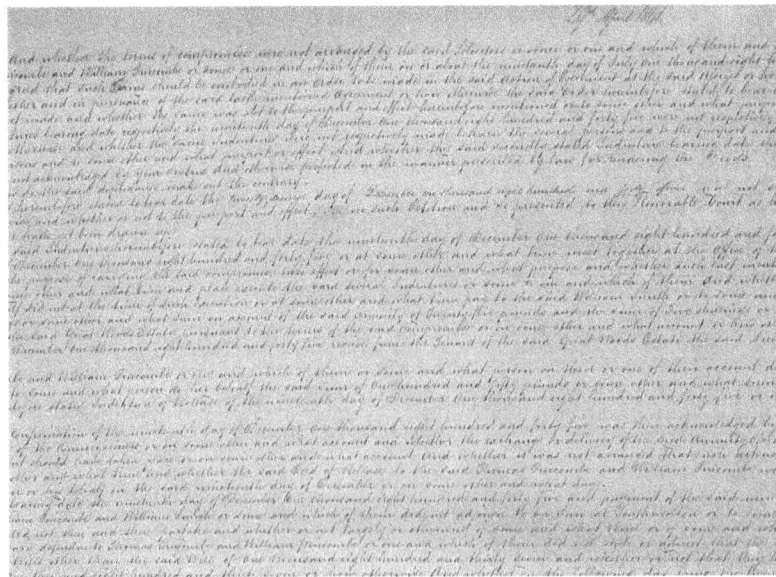

A small section of one page

The Chancery case was heard in South Molton. Although the Will had been proven some six years previously, Thomas said that this was handled under some duress. After the reading of the Will, on the day of John Pincombe's funeral but before it had been proven, his brother William, had started an 'Action of Ejectment'. This was to 'eject' Mary from 'Great Woods' and reclaim his own entitlement to the property, as 'heir at law'. William had then died in 1839, before it could be taken further. Thomas said that he had been pressed by some of the beneficiaries to settle the amounts due and had been advised by his solicitor to finalise the Will so that payments could be made. His solicitor had subsequently found the Will to be void, as one of the three signatories was not legally able to act as witness, his wife being the beneficiary of a small sum. The final judgement went in favour of Thomas, although Mary was awarded £150 and Thomas was charged with the court costs.

Following the court hearing, Thomas and his nephew William (William Pincombe's son), Mary and William Smith crossed over the road to the George Inn, to partake of some refreshment. Being a little loose of mouth, after a few drinks, Thomas and William said that it was lucky for them that the judge didn't know about the existence of a previous Will. Hearing this, William Smith instructed his solicitor to secure the earlier Will and begin court proceedings again. This time, the case was heard in Westminster.

William and Mary explained what had happened to the court and their wish for the earlier Will to be acted upon. Thomas Pincombe argued that Mary had been fully aware of all three Wills; dated March 1833, August 1834 and April 1837, when she signed the compromise agreement following the earlier hearing, it was therefore binding and the property legally his.

The Court of Chancery asked three main questions of all the witnesses:

1) Did they know the claimants, defenders and testator and for how long?
2) Were they at the funeral and what happened in respect of the Will reading?
3) Were they present when Mr Shapland valued items for sale and were the Wills discussed?

Thomas maintained that, following the funeral, Mary had selected the latest Will from a box containing all three Wills. She had then handed it to William Pincombe, telling him to read it. A week after the funeral, when Mr Shapland visited for valuation purposes, all three Wills were read over and discussed by everyone present, including Mary. Mary then took the box containing all three Wills to Mr Pearse, the family's solicitor. Thomas also maintained that, at the Inn, William had questioned him about the earlier Wills, asking where they were as he was interested in old documents (showing that he knew of their existence).

On another point, he said he had been accused of using John's money for his own gain, while acting as executor and trustee. He said that, on the contrary, there was not enough money to cover the settlement of John Pincombe's debts, funeral expenses and legacies.

A number of witnesses spoke out in favour of Mary's case:

Thomas Pincombe (son of John's brother Robert) said that at the funeral, only one Will was present and read.

Richard Pincombe (also Robert's son) said that he was residing at Great Woods from John's death until after the sale of items, some three months later. On the day of the funeral, William had taken the Will and read it. His brother John had expressed dissatisfaction, saying it couldn't be the right Will, but William said that it was and finished reading it. He was there when Mr Shapland visited the house and on no occasion were any Wills produced or discussed.

Sarah Ayre, who lived close to Great Woods, said she had shown Mr Shapland over the house and was not aware of any Wills being shared.

Ann Smalden, Mary's mother, said that William Pincombe had suggested delaying the reading of the Will until the following Sunday (the funeral was held on a Monday). John Pincombe (junior), along with others, objected, saying, 'No time like the present'. William then took the Will from a box belonging to John Pincombe (testator). On hearing it, John (junior) said he thought it was not John (senior)'s Will and William said that he knew of no other. George (another of Robert's sons) also said he never would have thought it was his uncle's Will. Some months later, when William Pincombe started the 'Action of Ejectment', Ann said she secured a copy of the Will from the solicitor, being unaware of any other.

The judgement was in favour of Mary and William. By the time the case was completed, Mary and William had three children, John, Mary and William. It had taken, from John's death in 1838, until 1850 to resolve.

North Devon, in the 1830s saw a growth in the number of its residents leaving to start new lives overseas. Locally, ships departed from Barnstaple, most bound for New York, St. Andrews (Newfoundland) and Montreal. The alternative was to sail from Plymouth. There were promises of better prospects in America and this was against a backdrop of growing unrest throughout rural southern England after a series of bad harvests. Parts of Kent had seen the worst of the demonstrations, including the destruction of new machinery, viewed by many farm labourers as depriving them of employment. The authorities were quick in their reaction and employed hundreds of special constables to restore order. Many were subsequently fined, imprisoned, transported or even executed. In Devon, the unrest was somewhat less. Having a higher number of small independent yeomen farmers, there had been no revolutionary change in the shape of the landscape and rural life. Nevertheless, it is known that 300 special constables were sworn in at Barnstaple.

The promise of a better life overseas, saw emigration continue throughout the 1840s and into the 1850s. Robert Pincombe (junior), son of Robert and Betty Pincombe (nee Rowcliffe) had left for the United States as the wave of emigration gathered pace and encouraged his siblings to join him. Their mother, Betty (Bill's 4xG Grandfather William's younger sister), had died in 1823 and their father, Robert (younger brother of my 4xG Grandfather John – the testator), had died four years later, in 1827. Robert (junior) had sold the land left to him by his father and had found life on the other side of the Atlantic to be particularly rewarding.

Whether it was Robert's enthusiasm for life overseas or the discomfort felt within the family due to an unpleasant court case that had lasted for more than a decade, sister Elizabeth and brothers John and Thomas all followed suit.

John Pincombe and his wife Elizabeth (nee Rew) set sail in November 1850 with their young son William. They disembarked in New York City in January 1851, travelled through New York State and crossed Niagara, finally arriving in Middlesex County, Canada, in the spring of 1851.

John Pincombe

Elizabeth (nee Pincombe) and her husband Richard Elsworthy, followed them to Canada, in 1855.

In the same year, Thomas made arrangements to take his wife and six children to Canada, where John had secured a home for them next to his own. They set sail aboard the 'John', a barque of 463 tons, bound for Quebec. There were 19 crew, 154 adult passengers, 98 children and 16 infants on board; a total of 287. Tragically, the ship struck the 'Manacles Rock', off St Keverne on the Cornish coast, just hours into their journey, with the loss of 195 lives. Thomas, his wife Sarah and all six of their children were drowned.

A commemorative plaque is in place on the outer wall of Molland Church. It tells of the loss of Thomas, Sarah and their young family: Jane, aged 13, Elizabeth, aged 11, Betsy, aged 9, Richard, aged 6, William, aged 4 and Mary, aged 1.

Of Robert and Betty's other children; brothers George, Richard and Philip remained in England, but by 1841 they had moved away from Devon, to Bristol, Gloucestershire, where they continued in dairy farming.

Philip remained in Gloucestershire, eventually settling in Clifton with his wife Julia. Their children were Charles, William, Emily and Mary. By 1851, Philip was a farmer of 90 acres.

Only Richard returned to Devon and was there in 1871, still a dairyman.

ERECTED
To the memory
and to record the disastrous death
of
THOMAS and SARAH PINCOMBE
of this Parish and their youthful
family of 6 sons and daughters
all of whom perished by shipwreck
together with 187 of their fellow
passengers.

The calamitous event happened on the Manacle rocks near St Keverne coast of Cornwall on the night of the 3rd of May 1855 within six hours after the lamented victims had left the harbour of Plymouth as Emigrants on their voyage to Quebec.

Come sudden death by flood or flame
Who trust in a Redeemer's name
Are still secure for thrones on high
And wait their entrance to the sky

William and Mary gave East Week to her mother Ann and step-father James. James farmed the land there until he retired. Thus, they lived next to Thomas Pincombe and his wife Philippa who farmed West Week! William and Mary themselves, kept the tenant farmers at Great Woods, providing a regular rental income. They lived in Salem Street, Barnstaple, where three further children were born: Ann, Jane and Tom. Then, in 1853, the family moved to Claverton Place, in Bath, where their youngest son, Arthur was born, totalling seven children in all.

By 1861, William had risen through the ranks and, in the Census, he described himself as Division Manager, Excise Branch of the Inland Revenue. Son John, aged 17, was a printer's apprentice and William, 14, a clerk in an attorney's office.

Mary died two years later, in 1863, aged only 43. She was buried at St Mark's Church, Lyncombe, Bath. Her gravestone tells of some sadness to follow. In the same grave is Tom, aged 13, Jane, aged 18 and Ann, aged 28, unmarried.

Their son, John, married Harriet, a young woman from Devon, and that is where they set up home. He gave up his ideas of being a printer and worked as a farm labourer at Dobbs Moor, Chumleigh, South Molton. John and Harriet had two sons, Frederick and Thomas, and a daughter, Laura. John would not see his young family grow up, however, as he died in 1875, the year Laura was born. Harriet, a young widow, had to return to live at her mother and step-father's home in Eggesford, Devon, with the children.

Mary and William's son William, also moved back to Devon, marrying Jane Incledon in 1866, in Heanton Punchardon, where she was born. By 1871, William was a Master Mariner and the couple had three young children: Frederick, Charles and Edith.

William (senior) remained at Claverton Place, working for the Inland Revenue, in Bath, where his daughters Mary and Ann looked after the house. His youngest son, Arthur, also still living at home, started to work as a shop assistant.

William died in 1871, aged 55, and he was buried with Mary, at St Mark's Church, in Lyncombe. His Will left everything to be shared equally between his children on the attainment of twenty-one years. So, the estate was held in trust and was finally sold in 1876, the time of Arthur's twenty-first birthday. Great Woods was sold to Nicholas Williams of Throck-Morton property. It remains part of the Throck-Morton Estate and is, still today, farmed by tenant farmers.

Great Woods, Molland, Devon

Bill and I visited Molland and as there was a sign advertising fresh eggs for sale at Great Woods, we knocked on the door. At the time of our visit, the current tenant farmers had been at the property for about ten years. Over the years they had seen a number of management changes and told us that Lady Mclaren Throck-Morton had recently passed away, leaving the estate to her daughter. They still weren't sure whether that would bring any further change but suggested that we might be able to find out more about the ancestral home at the estate office, just down the road, in Molland village. We did just that and found the office open. A lady at the desk asked if she could help, and I explained that we were trying to find out more about Great Woods, as it had been in our family during the 1800s. Another lady, who had been looking at a photograph with a local man, turned and informed me in no uncertain terms that that was impossible. In a very condescending manner, she told me that my family must have 'just been tenant farmers' as the whole of Molland had been in her family since the 1300s. We were obviously not going to find out any facts here! But, before leaving, I suggested that she might like to check the 1840 Tithe maps where it was very clear that Mary Pincombe Thorne was then the owner. The man followed us to the car and sold us one of his pictures – a very early photo of Molland.

Molland Village (late 1800s)

We continued past the site office and into the quaint little village, in the heart of which is the church of St Mary's. The church itself is rather unusual. Inside, the pews are set in what looks like long cubicles (with wooden doors and bolts at the aisle end). The wood surrounding the bench seat is almost at chest height, so that when seated, only the tallest of the congregation would have a good view of the altar.

Bill demonstrating the height of the wooden 'cubicles'

Molland Church Pew

St Mary's Church, Molland

The churchyard surrounds the church to three sides, with a pathway leading from front to back. It was from this path that we could see John Pincombe's grave.

Unusually, the engraver gives John's place of death: 'Woods Farm in this parish'.

On the sale of William's estate, there were four living beneficiaries. But his Will made clear that the children of a son or daughter who had predeceased him would be given their rightful share. John had died the year before the settlement. His widow Harriet remarried in 1883, a man called James Crocker. James was a flower grower/gardener. The couple, and the four children they had together following their marriage, lived in Exeter. In the Census of 1891, Harriet's mother and stepfather were listed as paupers, so it is perhaps unlikely that Harriet herself benefitted from William's Will.

So, what of John's children with Harriet?

Frederick John Smith married Jane Sellick and they too lived in Exeter. In 1911, their home 'Eagle Cottage', in Bonhay Road was also home to Jane's mother, brother and niece. The Census shows Frederick as the 'head' of the house and his profession as railway labourer.

Thomas and Laura, have proved more difficult to trace. In 1891, the Census shows Laura Smith, aged 17, a domestic servant in Exeter, but I have been unable to find anything beyond this date, or indeed for Thomas, married, single or deceased. It is impossible to verify whether John's children benefitted from William's Will, but in the case of Frederick, it is perhaps quite likely that his wishes were carried out.

Mary Smith was still unmarried in 1871, living at home where she, no doubt, was housekeeper for her father until his death.

William Smith (my 2xG Grandfather), as already mentioned, was married to Jane (nee Incledon). He was a Master Mariner in 1871, living in Heanton Punchardon, near Barnstaple. Soon after this, William, Jane and their four children; Frederick, Charles, Edith and John, moved to South Wales. William had found work that kept him closer to his growing family, as a Gas Works labourer. The Gas Industry in Glamorganshire was flourishing and he joined the Aberavon Gas Works at a time when it was expanding considerably. Thomas (my Great Grandfather) was born in Aberavon, in 1875. He was followed, about eighteen months later, by Albert Edward. Sadly, Albert died shortly after birth. William had developed skills in his new job that were very much at the 'cutting edge' of the time.

No doubt, with the aid of his inheritance, he was able to secure another position in Yatton, Somerset. By 1879, the family had settled in Yatton at the Gas Works Cottage, where William worked as a Gas Fitter. There they remained for the next thirty or more years, with William quickly rising to the position of Gas Manager. Frederick, Charles, Edith, John and Thomas, were joined by Louisa, Edward and Bertha to complete the family.

Ann Smith was 27 at the time of the property sale following her father William's death, but sadly, her life ended just a year later. She was unmarried and still lived at the family home.

William's youngest son, Arthur Smith also travelled to Devon. At the age of twenty-six he was a boarder at Churston Cottage, in Torquay. This was the home of Thomas Memery, an auctioneer, for whom he worked as a salesman. Arthur married Charlotte Crocker, in 1890. I feel that there is probably a connection between his wife, Charlotte, and John's widow Harriet's second husband, James Crocker, but as yet I have not found that link. Arthur emigrated to Australia, in 1898, travelling from Plymouth to Melbourne on the 'Oruba'. The journey took 75 days. Although the ship's records show that Arthur was a married man, he was travelling alone. This was a very common practice for those emigrating. The husband would leave first, to set up a home and work, with his wife and children following later. Arthur probably felt that with the additional financial stability he had, following his inheritance, they were in a particularly good position to set up in a new country.

The 1911 Census record, shows William and Jane Smith, with son Edward, still living at the Cottage on the Gas Works grounds. William, aged 66, is recorded as Gas Manager, and Edward, aged 30 and unmarried, is a Gas Stoker. The Yatton Local History Society, also shows the manager to be William as late as 1924, with his son Charles employed as the Gas Works secretary.

Jane died in 1922 and William followed, in 1927. They were buried in the churchyard of St Mary the Virgin, in the Parish of Yatton. The white headstone is 5.5ft in height (about 1.7m), with a flower motif inset at the head. It reads,

IN MEMORY OF
JANE
THE BELOVED WIFE OF
WILLIAM SMITH
WHO PASSED PEACEFULLY TO HER REST
ON THE MORNING OF
FEBRUARY 25TH 1922
IN HER 84TH YEAR
PEACE PERFECT PEACE
ALSO
WILLIAM SMITH
WHO DIED JUNE 8TH 1927
AGED 82 YEARS

Thomas Smith

Thomas and his younger sister Louisa, left for Acton, West London, before 1901. Thomas found work as a clerk and Louisa as a bookseller and stationer. Their mother, Jane, was visiting them at the time of the 1901 Census. Three and a half miles away, twenty-one-year-old Rose Berridge, worked as a housemaid for Thomas and Mary Dodd, in Kensington…

The Incledons

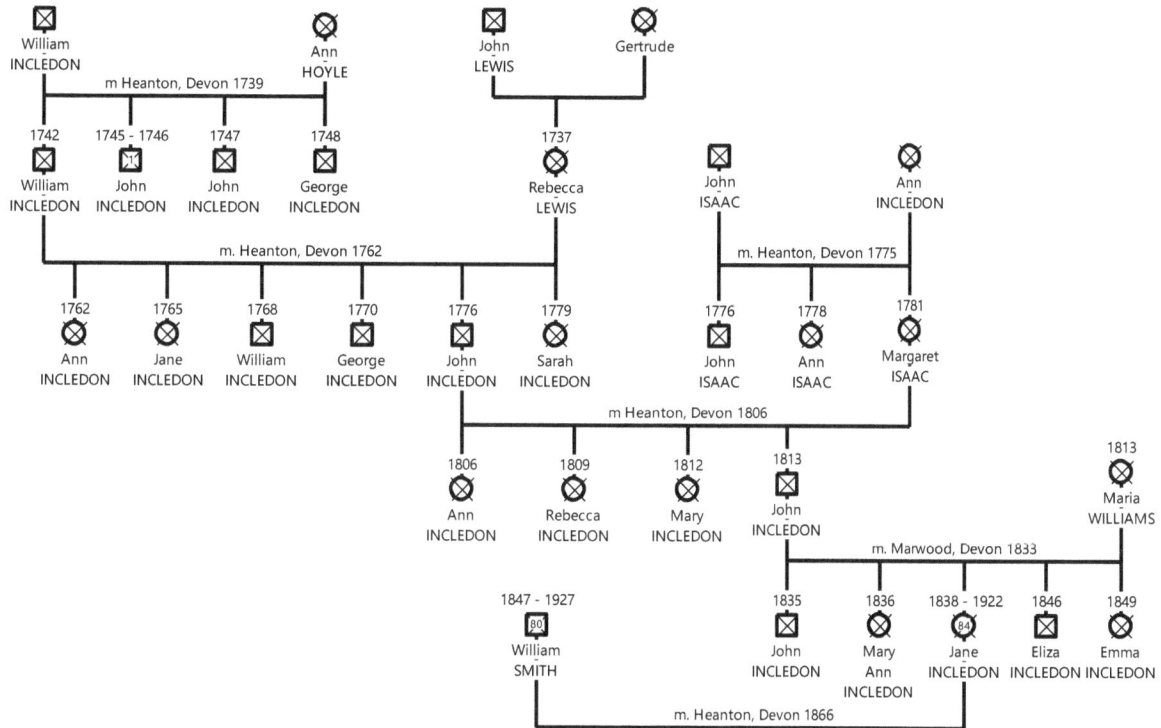

Family tree diagram:

- William INCLEDON — m Heanton, Devon 1739 — Ann HOYLE
  - 1742 William INCLEDON
  - 1745 - 1746 John INCLEDON
  - 1747 John INCLEDON
  - 1748 George INCLEDON
- John LEWIS — Gertrude
  - 1737 Rebecca LEWIS

William INCLEDON (1742) — m. Heanton, Devon 1762 — Rebecca LEWIS (1737)
  - 1762 Ann INCLEDON
  - 1765 Jane INCLEDON
  - 1768 William INCLEDON
  - 1770 George INCLEDON
  - 1776 John INCLEDON
  - 1779 Sarah INCLEDON

John ISAAC — m. Heanton, Devon 1775 — Ann INCLEDON
  - 1776 John ISAAC
  - 1778 Ann ISAAC
  - 1781 Margaret ISAAC

John INCLEDON (1776) — m Heanton, Devon 1806 — Margaret ISAAC (1781)
  - 1806 Ann INCLEDON
  - 1809 Rebecca INCLEDON
  - 1812 Mary INCLEDON
  - 1813 John INCLEDON

John INCLEDON (1813) — m. Marwood, Devon 1833 — 1813 Maria WILLIAMS
  - 1835 John INCLEDON
  - 1836 Mary Ann INCLEDON
  - 1838 - 1922 Jane INCLEDON (84)
  - 1846 Eliza INCLEDON
  - 1849 Emma INCLEDON

1847 - 1927 William SMITH (80) — m. Heanton, Devon 1866 — Jane INCLEDON (1838 - 1922)

Incledon, is an ancient estate in the parish of Braunton, North Devon. It gave its name to the locally prominent 'de Incledon' (now Incledon, pronounced Ingleton) family. The estate was first recorded in 1160 and is situated one mile north-west of St Brannock's Church in Braunton. In 1319, the Incledon family purchased the estate of Buckland, and the present Georgian Buckland House, which is half a mile south-east of Incledon, was still occupied in 2014 by descendants of the Incledon-Webber family.

The earliest of our Incledon forebears that I have been able to find are William and Ann, my 6xG Grandparents. William Incledon and Ann Hoyle married in 1739, in Heanton Punchardon, about a mile south-east of Braunton. They had three sons, William, John and George, and a further son, John, who died in infancy. Their eldest son, William, married Rebecca Lewis, daughter of John and Gertrude, another local family. They followed tradition with the naming of their children: Ann, Jane, William, George, John and Sarah. It would appear that the family were well educated, with George becoming an assistant surgeon, and subsequently, his son Frederick achieving a Batchelor of the Arts at Cambridge University. John, my 4xG Grandfather, was a mason. He may have provided some of the gravestones in the churchyard of St Augustine, in Heanton Punchardon. It is here, in fact, that the graves of George's daughters, Agnes and Ann, and John now lie.

John married Margaret Isaac, at the church, in 1806. Margaret was the daughter of John Isaac and Ann Incledon. My research points towards Ann being a daughter of William Incledon and Ann Hoyle, making John and Margaret first cousins, but final proof of this has not been possible thus far. They had four children, Ann (Margaret's mother's name), Rebecca (John's mother's name), Mary (strangely not Margaret, after her own mother) and John (after his father).

John became a sexton. He would also have worked at the church of St Augustine, in Heanton Punchardon, charged with the maintenance of its buildings and the surrounding graveyard. John married Maria Williams, in 1833, in the nearby village of Marwood. It was one of their five children, Jane Incledon who married William Smith, at St Augustine's Church, in 1866, and would become my Great Grandmother.

St Augustine's Church, Heanton Punchardon

The Berridges

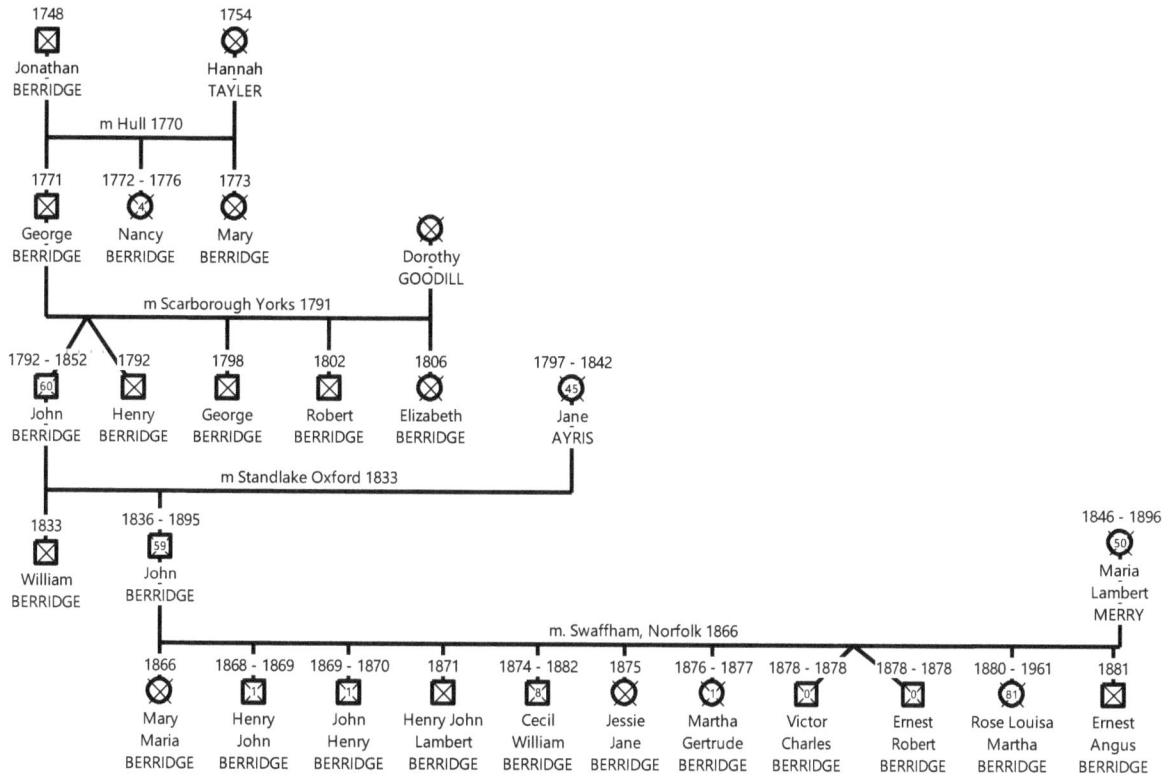

1748
Jonathan BERRIDGE

1754
Hannah TAYLER

m Hull 1770

1771
George BERRIDGE

1772 - 1776
Nancy BERRIDGE

1773
Mary BERRIDGE

Dorothy GOODILL

m Scarborough Yorks 1791

1792 - 1852
John BERRIDGE

1792
Henry BERRIDGE

1798
George BERRIDGE

1802
Robert BERRIDGE

1806
Elizabeth BERRIDGE

1797 - 1842
Jane AYRIS

m Standlake Oxford 1833

1833
William BERRIDGE

1836 - 1895
John BERRIDGE

1846 - 1896
Maria Lambert MERRY

m. Swaffham, Norfolk 1866

1866
Mary Maria BERRIDGE

1868 - 1869
Henry John BERRIDGE

1869 - 1870
John Henry BERRIDGE

1871
Henry John Lambert BERRIDGE

1874 - 1882
Cecil William BERRIDGE

1875
Jessie Jane BERRIDGE

1876 - 1877
Martha Gertrude BERRIDGE

1878 - 1878
Victor Charles BERRIDGE

1878 - 1878
Ernest Robert BERRIDGE

1880 - 1961
Rose Louisa Martha BERRIDGE

1881
Ernest Angus BERRIDGE

The earliest Berridges in our family that I have been able to find are Jonathan, born in 1748, and his wife Hannah Taylor. They were married at the Holy Trinity Church in Hull, in the East Riding of Yorkshire, in 1770; Hannah was just sixteen. The couple had three children in quick succession: George in 1771, Nancy in 1772 and Mary in 1773. Sadly, in the year of Mary's birth, Jonathan died. How Hannah managed to cope we cannot know, at the age of nineteen, she had three very young children and was dealing with the loss of her husband. If family were unable to help, the only support in the area would seem to have been at 'Charity Hall' the workhouse of Kingston-Upon-Hull that took inmates from those in need in Hannah's parish. If Hannah and the children did enter the workhouse, where it was more difficult to control the spread of infection, it may account for the tragedy that followed three years later, when four-year-old Nancy and three-year-old Mary both died. It is likely that young George would have joined the workforce at around the age of twelve, helping Hannah to start afresh. Hannah finally remarried, at the age of thirty, when George was thirteen.

George took up work as a Chaise Driver. This would have been a small single horse drawn carriage for transporting one or two people. His work may well have taken him from district to district, within Yorkshire.

At the age of twenty, he married Dorothy Goodill, in Scarborough, Yorkshire. The couple set up home in Bishop Burton and just a year after their marriage, Dorothy gave birth to twin boys, John and Henry. They were strong, and, unlike many twin births of the time, the boys survived childhood, living to have families of their own. Three further children were born to George and Dorothy: George, Robert and Elizabeth.

Henry remained in Bishop Burton, where he married and had a daughter, Mary, named after her mother. Henry worked as a groom on an estate. His twin brother, John, travelled south and met his wife in Ducklington, Oxford. He was almost forty when he married Jane Ayris. Jane was a local woman whose family all appear to have been in service, working and living at the Barley Park Lodge Estate. Ducklington, was an area made up mostly of farm land, with the majority of residents working in jobs associated with arable and sheep farming. Much of the work was limited to the summer months, the cause of a great deal of hardship at other times of the year. The 1841 Census shows Jane Berridge's occupation as butcher, living at Barley Park Lodge with her two children, William aged 7 and John aged 4. A number of other Ayris family members can also be spotted. Jane's husband, John, is not listed, and I have yet to find him in the Census records for 1841.

Jane died the following year and this appears to have necessitated a split in the family. By 1851, her husband John was living with his widowed brother-in-law, Percival Walsh, a retired Attorney's Solicitor. John was working as a Hatter.

Coleshill House, Berkshire

Their son William, had taken a position at Coleshill House, in Berkshire (now Oxfordshire, since a change of boundaries), as footman.

Youngest son John, aged fourteen, was living with his widowed uncle, William Baston, a Miller, and his family of similarly-aged children. Young John, was working as an errand boy.

The households of Percival Walsh and William Baston must have seemed in such contrast to what John and his son John had been used to. Percival and William were both men of some standing and employed servants in their homes. What was particularly fortuitous for them was that the houses were next-door-but-one from each other, in Stanton Harcourt, Oxfordshire. I think that John (the elder) may have been suffering poorer health, leading to the change from more physical work to work that could be predominantly sedentary. He died the year after the Census, in 1852.

John continued in service and moved to Lincolnshire, where he took a position at Belvoir Castle. He became a 'Household Servant'. Over time, records show him working also as a Porter and Footman, like his brother William. At Belvoir Castle, John was one of a number of footmen. This perhaps, tells a little of John and William's appearance, because footmen tended to be chosen for their looks and height. Amongst the gentry, footmen represented a status symbol. Apparently, taller footmen were paid higher wages, and the best status symbol of wealth was to have footmen who matched in height and looks. The livery they wore, was in a style more popular a century earlier, often including knee breeches, silk stockings and braided coats. Their job seems chiefly to have been conspicuously waiting, wherever their services might be needed at a moment's notice. Behind the scenes, they also took on a range of tasks such as polishing silverware, cleaning shoes and boots and riding on the back of coaches.

Belvoir Castle, Lincolnshire

In 1859, John became a paid-up member of Oddfellows, a friendly society that had finally been given legal status in 1851. There being no National Insurance to protect income in times of illness or injury, by joining a friendly society, workers could protect themselves and their families against those perils. The Redmile Archive web site has uncovered an old photograph, thought to have been taken around 1880, of Oddfellows members who met at the Windmill Inn. The men are all wearing sashes and holding maces. Unfortunately, it is too unclear to identify individuals. The membership book confirms John's membership and shows the majority of other members coming from Redmile with a number also from Belvoir Castle.

Meanwhile, at Redmile, others in service included two sisters: Maria and Christiana Lambert. The girls were employed in domestic service. John, aged 21 and Maria, aged 20, met and perhaps rather too quickly, she found she was pregnant. Maria returned to her home town, Gooderstone, in Norfolk, where the couple married, at St George's Church, just weeks before the birth of their daughter Mary. Following their marriage, Maria continued to live at Redmile, and John kept his job as footman, presumably, living at Redmile when off duty. The 1871 Census, shows Maria, still at Redmile, with their four-year-old daughter. At the time of the Census, Mary's eleven-year-old sister, Ruth Lambert, was staying with her, but probably just for a visit, as she was still at school. These living arrangements were only to be a temporary measure though, as John and Maria returned to live in Gooderstone before the birth of their son, Henry, in 1872.

There may well have been more than tradition in naming their baby son after Maria's father. Henry Lambert had been a tenant farmer of 40 acres and keeper of a Beer House, in Gooderstone. He generously gave the pub to John and Maria, both as home and income, from the time they returned to Gooderstone. He also reduced the land he was farming to 12 acres. At the same time John started to farm, and by 1881, he was recorded as Innkeeper and farmer of 78 acres, employing one man. John changed the name of the beer house, from Jessop's (the man who started it in 1851) to The Cricketer's Inn, and it was here the family stayed for the rest of John's life. For a young man who had grown up in service, knowing little of family life following the death of his mother when he was just six years old, this must have been a dream come true. To have a family of his own (and, it appears, a supportive extended family), a secure home and to be master within his working life, was I'm sure something that he never considered a possibility.

John and Maria had eleven children, four daughters and seven sons. Sadly, only five survived infancy: Mary, Henry, Jessie, Rose and Ernest. Unfortunately, just as Maria had experienced before her, Mary became pregnant before she married. She gave birth, at the age of 21, to a daughter, Gertrude. There being only six years between Maria and John's youngest, Ernest, and little Gertrude, they decided to raise their grand-daughter as their own. Three years later, Mary went on to marry a local gamekeeper, George Pryke, and the couple moved to Shropshire to bring up a growing family.

John died in 1895, aged 59. Maria took over the running of the Cricketer's Inn, but must have found it a struggle, for a new licensee was in place by 1900. Sadly, she was back into service again, but this time with Gertrude. They moved to Hammersmith and worked as domestic housemaids. Gertrude was to continue as a housemaid, working for households in the affluent Kensington area of London. For a while, it appears that she adopted the name Lillian Gertrude Berridge, or perhaps she was known as Lily in her position as servant and the head of house recorded her details inaccurately. My aunt remembers her 'aunt' Gertie fondly, and was aware of some family utterings about the circumstances of her birth.

John and Maria's children were grown and beginning to make their own way in life.

Henry moved to London, where he became a police constable with the Metropolitan Police. He married, Kate, a young woman from Lymington, Hampshire, and they settled in Wood Green, London.

Jessie married Walter Blacker, another gamekeeper. For a while they lived in Wrexham, where their only son was born, but they then returned to Norfolk, and settled in Kings Lynn. It was lovely to see that Rose Pryke, their niece, was visiting at the time of the 1901 Census.

Ernest, left Norfolk for Marylebone, initially securing a job as stableman. He then joined the Metropolitan Police, just as his brother Henry had done. In 1911, he was living at a police house in Tooting, with several other single police constables. He married Georgina Vickers, in 1921.

Rose Smith (nee Berridge)

Rose, my Great Grandmother, also went to London and, as was the case with most young women without independent means, she went into service. She worked as a housemaid for a couple named Dodd. Her employer was described as a 'job master', with a house in Gloucester Walk, Kensington. She met Thomas Smith, who was by then, working as a clerk not far from the house. Unfortunately, for the couple, like Rose's mother and sister, Rose found herself pregnant before their marriage, which took place in July, 1903. The wedding was held at St Paul's, Onslow Square, in South Kensington. Rose's brother Ernest and her 'sister' Gertrude were both there and signed as witnesses to the marriage. The certificate shows that Thomas and Rose were both living at 14, Neville Street, in Kensington, at the time. They must have moved, however, because Donald was born in Chelsea, towards the end of the same year. In all, Rose and Thomas had eight children.

Rose was an amazing cook and would turn her hand to any recipe on the old range cooker. The aroma of baking perpetually present in her kitchen where she would always have sausage rolls and Garibaldi biscuits for family and visitors. So good were her apple pies, that throughout my childhood (and beyond) she was known as 'Apple-Pie Nanny'.

Rose was not a lover of change. She was decidedly aggrieved when the boys treated her to a new cooker and when the gas mantles were replaced with electric lights.

Rose (nee Berridge) and Thomas Smith's Family c. 1911 children are: Donald, Milly, Douglas and Eric

She loved children and had taken a key role in caring for her daughter Doreen's eldest daughter, so the couple could manage work. When Doreen and her husband Joe decided to move to Ireland, Rose was so distraught and the child so attached to her, that the decision was made to make Rose's caring role a permanent one. Her grand-daughter stayed with Rose until she married.

Thomas, was a man with a shed! Rather a 'glory hole' full of 'useful' old tools and off-cuts that you simply could not be without. My mother recalls that if anyone mentioned a need for something like nails or materials, his response was always 'I've got hundreds of those in the shed'. He'd then disappear for some significant time, usually returning with a handful of rusty or bent items, of little use for the intended task. Rose would then declare, 'Silly old fool!' referring to her husband.

When reminiscing, Elaine (my mother) and her sister, Diana, remembered fondly their grandfather Thomas's attempts at mending things. Thomas was apparently a clever man, but his do-it-yourself solutions were inexpensive and practical, rather than inobtrusive and aesthetically pleasing. The chair leg was mended, with the unsightly addition of a splint of wood bound with rope. The broken door latch was held in an open position by nailing a strip of leather from the front of the door to the back, across the latch. 'So much quieter!', he declared as it wedged into the door frame.

He always had a pipe and was frequently singeing his trousers with hot ash, needing to pat his legs to put out the smouldering fabric. Apparently, on one occasion he actually set his trousers on fire!

A lovely man, he could also be somewhat tactless. When he noticed that my cousin, a very settled, 'good' baby, hardly cried, he pronounced, 'She'll not live, babies always cry. She'll not live.' Not what any new mother needed to hear, it was fortunate that my aunt knew him well.

Milly and Douglas, like Donald, were born in Chelsea. Eric, Bernard (Berny), Kenneth (Kenny), Walter (Wally) and Doreen, were born in Battersea, following a move to 52, Orbel Street.

Donald Incledon Smith

Donald became a restaurant owner. Sadly, he died aged 46.

Kenny, Berny, Douglas and Wally Smith

The remaining sons all went into the car trade, based mainly in the south London area.

Milly and Leslie Frankland with Elaine and Diana

Milly married Leslie Frankland and settled in the Battersea area of London. They had daughters Jean, Elaine and Diana.

Douglas and Cissie Smith

Douglas and Doris Smith

Douglas married Cissie and they had two daughters. Later, he married Doris and had two sons.

Eric Campbell Smith

Eric married Dora and had a son and a daughter.

Kenny married Winnie and had three children; two daughters and a son.

Kenneth William Smith

Berny married Dorothy, and later, following her death, he married Jean. He had one son.

Walter Smith

Wally, married Enid, and later, Betty. Wally and Betty had six children, sadly losing one in infancy.

Doreen (Tiny) Smith

Doreen would always be known as 'Tiny', because she was so small as a young girl. I would think, however, that a little girl born after a succession of strapping lads would be likely to appear rather delicate and petite!

'Tiny' married Joe and settled in Ireland. They had eight children, four sons and four daughters.

The Lamberts

Edward LAMBERT — Mary

1786	1787	1790	1793	1794	1796	1796	1797	1797	1798	1799	1800	1802	1803	1804	1805
Edward LAMBERT	George LAMBERT	William LAMBERT	Rebecca LAMBERT	Lydia LAMBERT	Edward LAMBERT	Elizabeth LAMBERT	Mary LAMBERT	Edward LAMBERT	Stephen LAMBERT	Stephen LAMBERT	Lydia LAMBERT	Sophia LAMBERT	Stephen Hubbard LAMBERT	John LAMBERT	Sarah LAMBERT

1763 John MERRY — 1787 Hannah LYON
m. Chatteris, Cambridge 1806

William LAMBERT — m Gooderstone, Norfolk 1800

1790 Margaret HEATH

1763 - 1809 William WARNER — 1791 George SEPPINGS — 1785 - 1851 Jane BODY
m. Norfolk 1812

1807 - 1810	1810	1812	1814 - 1846	1825 - 1825	1827 - 1837
William MERRY	Martha Lyon MERRY	Hannah MERRY	William Lyon MERRY	James Lyon MERRY	Mary Ann MERRY

1802	1804	1806	1808	1811	1813 - 1890	1815	1818
John LAMBERT	Mary LAMBERT	Josiah LAMBERT	Frances LAMBERT	Robert LAMBERT	Henry LAMBERT	Maria LAMBERT	Sarah LAMBERT

1805	1808 - 1808	1819	1816
John WARNER	Mary WARNER	Mary SEPPINGS	Osborn SEPPINGS

m Hilborough, Norfolk 1837   m Swaffham, Norfolk 1851

1836 - 1895	1837	1840	1841	1844	1846 - 1896	1849 - 1879	1852	1859
John BERRIDGE	Jane MERRY	William MERRY	Mary Ann MERRY	Margaret Lambert MERRY	Maria Lambert MERRY	Christiana Lambert MERRY	Hagar LAMBERT	Ruth LAMBERT

m. Swaffham, Norfolk 1866

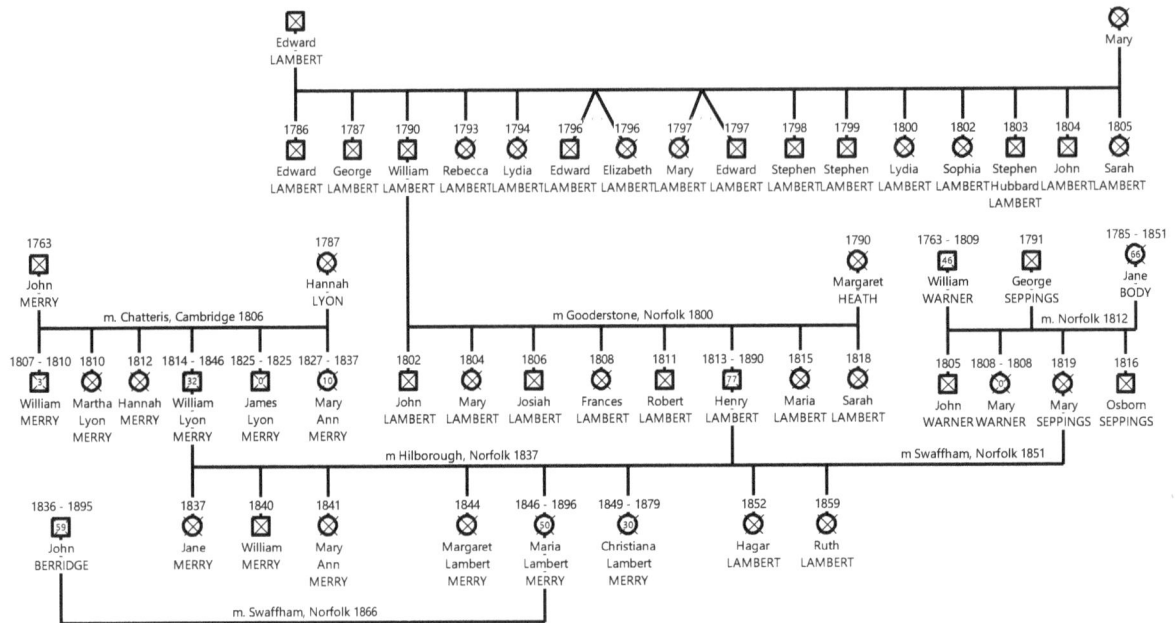

Tracing the Lamberts, initially, caused some consternation. Records such as Maria and John Berridge's marriage licence recorded her as Maria Lambert. However, the parish record of her baptism has her name as Maria Lambert Merry. Well, the homework has been done and the sorry tale can now be told…

Gooderstone, in Norfolk, was home to a number of generations of Lamberts, mainly involved in farming and inn-keeping. The earliest Lambert that I have been able to trace in our family, was Edward, born about 1750. He and his wife Mary had an amazing seventeen children, over a period of nineteen years. These included two sets of fraternal twins. A closer look at their names, however, shows three Edwards, three Stephens and two Lydias, it is clear that the couple had suffered many bereavements amongst their infant children.

Their son William Lambert, was the first recorded innkeeper of 'The Three Tuns', an Inn in 'The Street', Gooderstone. Subsequently, William's son Josiah was innkeeper of 'The Swan Inn', right in the centre of Gooderstone. The Inn remained in his family from before 1841 until 1912.

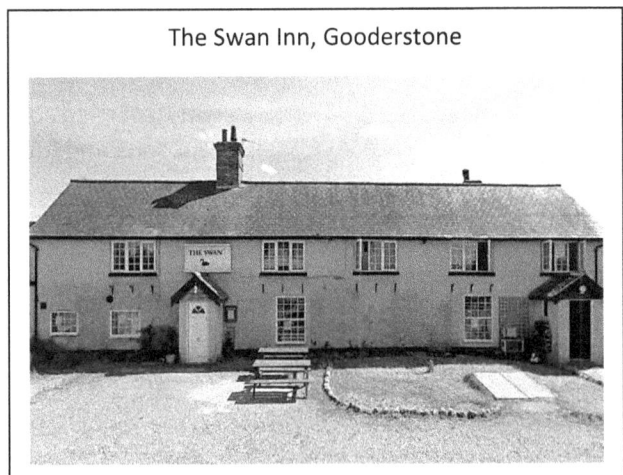

The Swan Inn, Gooderstone

Meanwhile, Josiah's brother Henry Lambert was keeper of the 'Beer House' in Hilborough Road, also in Gooderstone, from 1869. This would change its name to 'The Cricketer's,' in 1880.

Bill and I visited the 'Swan Inn', in Gooderstone, which is still a popular village pub and has probably changed little over the years. Neither of the other pubs are in existence today.

Just opposite the 'Swan' is St George's parish church. A stroll around the churchyard revealed a number of Lambert graves, proof of the family having lived and worked in the area for a long time.

St George's Church, Gooderstone

In 1841, Henry was 25 years old and living in a lodging house. Next door, was Josiah and his family, already listed as 'innkeeper'.

Meanwhile...

A short distance away, in Hilborough, 25-year-old William Merry, was living with his wife Mary (nee Seppings) and two of their children, William (aged 2) and Mary (a baby). Their four-year-old daughter Jane was staying with Mary's parents, in Hilborough.

William was a miller. He had married Mary on 26th January, four years earlier. Mary was only seventeen and heavily pregnant. She gave birth about five weeks later, to a baby girl, Jane. This would have been a difficult start for any marriage.

It is not clear how Henry met Mary Merry, but a child was born to Mary, named Margaret, in 1843. The place of birth was Gooderstone, not Hilborough. Given all the known facts, it can probably be assumed that Mary was living with Henry. Margaret was baptised Margaret Lambert, but her birth certificate names her Margaret Lambert Merry. The space for father's name is left empty. Margaret's birth was followed two years later by the arrival of Maria, and then three years after that, by the arrival of Christiana. All three girls had Lambert as a middle name on their birth certificate but were baptised without the additional name.

Henry and Mary, probably hadn't heard of William Merry's death. Mary's husband William had been staying with his brother in Cambridgeshire and suffered, what was to prove to be, a fatal intussusception of the intestine. He died in 1846, before Maria's birth and well before Christiana's birth.

At the time of the 1851 Census, the couple had heard the news, as Mary was recorded as a widow. The Census records her as living with Henry, in Gooderstone village, as 'housekeeper'. At the time,

Henry was a farmer and Mary's son William Merry, at eleven years old, was working with him as an agricultural labourer. It was in the same year, that Henry and Mary finally married.

It is the 1861 Census that gives the true parentage of the children. The relationship to the head of the house, Henry, is clearly written. Mary and William's daughter Mary Merry, is 'step-daughter', Margaret Lambert, Maria Lambert and Christiana Lambert, are 'daughters' and then the children born since the marriage, Hagan Lambert and Ruth Lambert, are also 'daughters'. None of Henry's daughters had retained the 'Merry' name. Interestingly, a baby, Georgiana Merry, is amongst their number and would appear to be the child of unmarried Mary Merry (aged 20).

When the Jessop's Beer House, was advertised for sale, along with six acres of land, Henry completed the purchase. He already had some experience of the running of public houses from his father and brother's endeavours. The land would extend his existing farm holding.

Two further children joined the Lambert family: Henry Theophilus, born in 1864 and Jessie, born in 1881. Henry (known as Theophilus to avoid confusion) is described as 'grandson' in 1871, but 'son' in 1881. It is likely that he was the son of William and his wife Jane Dixon but raised by his grandparents. Jessie is the likely son of unmarried Ruth. He was only two months old at the time of the 1881 census, and 23-year-old Ruth was the only daughter at home with her parents.

Over time, Henry and Mary's children grew and left home. Maria and Christiana had been in service together in Leicestershire. They both returned to Gooderstone, where Maria, married to John Berridge, brought up her family. Christiana died, unmarried, aged 30. Hagar married Henry Dodd, a farmer, and remained in Gooderstone. Ruth married Thomas Norman, a warrener and also remained in the area. She took over the care of her nephew Theophilus, by then an agricultural labourer.

So, back to my Great Great Grandmother, Maria. She was registered at birth Maria Lambert Merry, because her mother Mary was still married to William Merry (although, unknown at the time, William had already died). There is no doubt that her biological father was Henry Lambert. After Henry and Mary's marriage, all of his natural children assumed his name. By the time Maria married John Berridge, she was only known as Maria Lambert, and that is the name on the marriage certificate and it is the way she signed herself.

The Willis and Bartlett Families

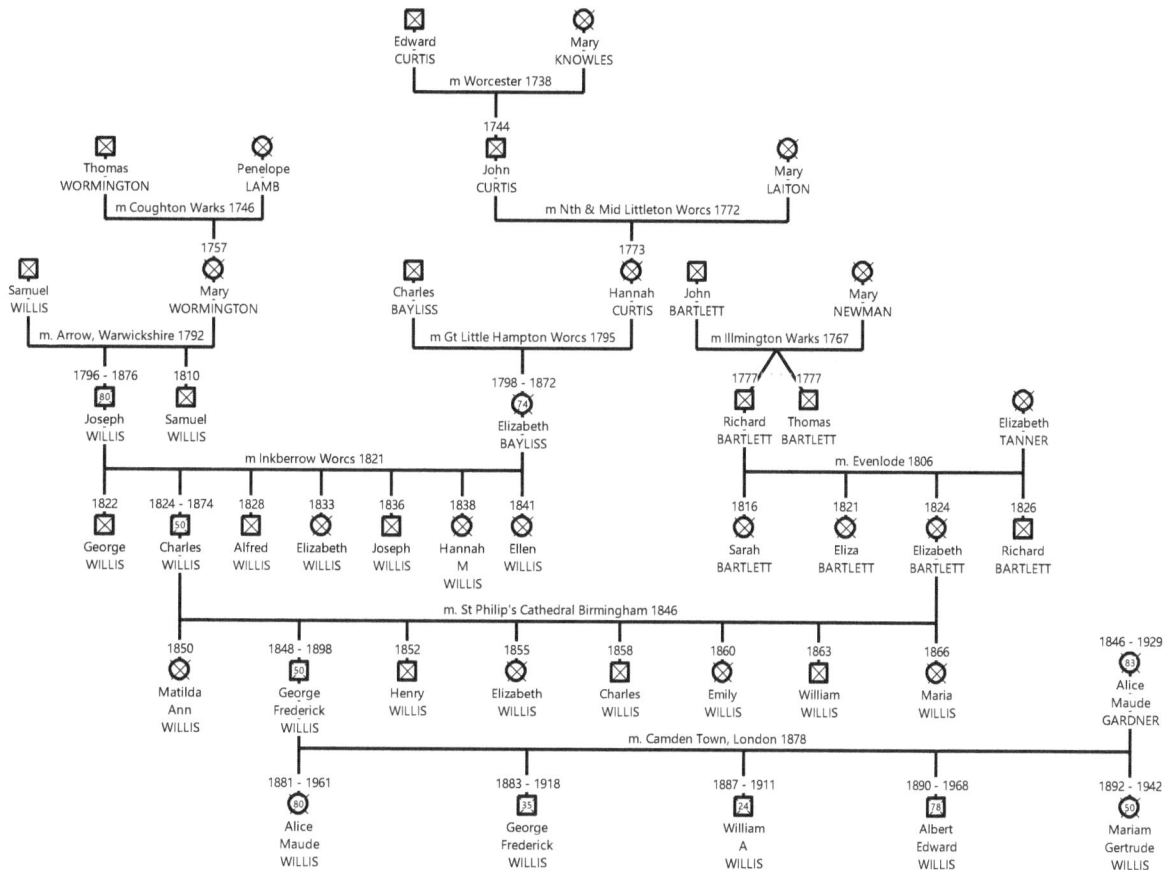

Edward CURTIS — Mary KNOWLES — m Worcester 1738
- 1744 John CURTIS — m Nth & Mid Littleton Worcs 1772 — Mary LAITON
  - 1773 Hannah CURTIS

Thomas WORMINGTON — Penelope LAMB — m Coughton Warks 1746
- 1757 Mary WORMINGTON

Samuel WILLIS — Mary WORMINGTON — m. Arrow, Warwickshire 1792
- 1796 – 1876 Joseph WILLIS (80)
- 1810 Samuel WILLIS

Charles BAYLISS — m Gt Little Hampton Worcs 1795
- 1798 – 1872 Elizabeth BAYLISS (74)

John BARTLETT — Mary NEWMAN — m Illmington Warks 1767
- 1777 Richard BARTLETT
- 1777 Thomas BARTLETT — m. Evenlode 1806 — Elizabeth TANNER

Joseph WILLIS & Elizabeth BAYLISS — m Inkberrow Worcs 1821:
- 1822 George WILLIS
- 1824 – 1874 Charles WILLIS (50)
- 1828 Alfred WILLIS
- 1833 Elizabeth WILLIS
- 1836 Joseph WILLIS
- 1838 Hannah M WILLIS
- 1841 Ellen WILLIS

Thomas BARTLETT & Elizabeth TANNER:
- 1816 Sarah BARTLETT
- 1821 Eliza BARTLETT
- 1824 Elizabeth BARTLETT
- 1826 Richard BARTLETT

Charles WILLIS & Elizabeth BARTLETT — m. St Philip's Cathedral Birmingham 1846:
- 1850 Matilda Ann WILLIS
- 1848 – 1898 George Frederick WILLIS (50)
- 1852 Henry WILLIS
- 1855 Elizabeth WILLIS
- 1858 Charles WILLIS
- 1860 Emily WILLIS
- 1863 William WILLIS
- 1866 Maria WILLIS

George Frederick WILLIS & Alice Maude GARDNER (1846 – 1929, 83) — m. Camden Town, London 1878:
- 1881 – 1961 Alice Maude WILLIS (80)
- 1883 – 1918 George Frederick WILLIS (35)
- 1887 – 1911 William A WILLIS (24)
- 1890 – 1968 Albert Edward WILLIS (78)
- 1892 – 1942 Mariam Gertrude WILLIS (50)

The earliest Willis came from Fenny Compton, in Warwickshire, in around 1350. Our own direct ancestors, are indeed in this area, but so far, I have only been able to go back to the mid 1700s. Samuel Willis starts our tree, married to Mary Wormington, they married and settled in Arrow, Warwickshire, just south of Birmingham. It is their son Joseph, born four years after their marriage, in 1796, that is my 3xG Grandfather. Joseph was a gardener. He married a young woman, Elizabeth Bayliss, from just over the border in Worcestershire, her home town of Inkberrow being five miles from Arrow. The couple moved to Birmingham where they had seven children: four boys and three girls.

Joseph changed occupation from gardener to butcher, but then back to gardening again, clearly his job of choice. Neither of these occupations interested his sons. The eldest son, George, had shown from quite an early age a liking for jewellery making. He set himself up as a jeweller, in Birmingham. Joseph's second son, Charles, became a glass cutter.

Alfred, two years younger than Charles, started working life as a porter, but moved on to coffee-roasting and set himself up as a coffee dealer (he must have been ahead of his time!). The youngest of the sons, Joseph, after his father, was a gun-maker. The daughters, Elizabeth, Hannah and Ellen, all worked in card-cutting and paper staining, until their marriages.

Clearly, Joseph and Elizabeth's children were all creatively talented. All credit to the couple for the nurture and encouragement they must have shown to the youngsters as they grew up, allowing them to develop in their own areas of interest.

St Philip's Cathedral, Birmingham

Charles married Elizabeth Bartlett, daughter of Richard Bartlett, a carpenter. Their wedding, in 1846, was at St Philip's Cathedral, in Birmingham.

The couple's first home was in Icknield Street, the street still lived in by Charles' mother and father, as well as the younger members of the family. Here, they had all eight children: Matilda, George, Henry, Elizabeth, Charles, Emily, William and Maria. It must have been lovely for the children growing up, to have their grandparents and aunts so close.

The family moved for a while to Dudley, in Staffordshire, where all the boys followed their father into glass-cutting, but this heralded a major change for them. Following the loss of Joseph and Elizabeth, who must have played a big part in all their lives, Charles and Elizabeth moved the family to Hampstead, London. Charles and his sons may have felt that the particular skills they had developed could perhaps be put to more lucrative use. Tragically, just a short while after their life-changing move, life took another unanticipated turn. In 1874, Charles died.

With their experience of glass-cutting, the brothers, had developed their skills towards more specialist lens cutting, for spectacle-making. Over the next years they described themselves as opticians and specialised in the production of gold spectacles, for the wealthier customers.

Alice (nee Gardner) and George Willis

George met and married Alice Gardner, a native Londoner, and they moved into lodgings not far from the rest of the family. Their first-born, a daughter, was named after her mother, but given a middle name by which she was known. So, she was Alice Maude, known all her life as Maude. This was becoming quite commonplace, allowing children to be named after their parents, but hoping to avoid the likely confusion. They had five children in all: Alice Maude (Maude), George Frederick, William Arthur, Albert Edward and Mariam Gertrude (Gert).

From their arrival in London, George's brothers, sisters and his mother, had lived at 2, Erskine Mews, Hampstead. As soon as they were able, George and his young family moved to be closer to them. This probably would have helped the brothers to develop their family business but would also emulate the closeness of family that George himself had known as a child. Their new address was 10, Erskine Mews.

Henry and George, continued in the optician business, but times were changing. The business was not destined to pass from father to son, as they might have hoped. The introduction of more automated manufacturing of spectacle frames, as well as more stringent training for those offering diagnostics, may have brought about an end to the demand for their particular skills. Their brother Charles started to work as a painter and William became a bar-tender.

Alice Maude Willis

Alice Willis (nee Gardner) and daughters Gert (left) and Maude (right)

So, none of George and Alice's own children would follow their father into optician work. Maude went into service, where she worked as a housemaid. The house was that of August Wolff, a German leather merchant, his wife and three children. Situated in Belsize Avenue, it was a substantial house with a staff of ten, made up of two cook/domestics, one kitchen maid, one under housemaid, one nurse/domestic, one hospital trained nurse, one parlour maid and three housemaids.

George Frederick Willis

George became a horse-keeper. This is almost certainly how he met his wife, Jane Susan Pereira, since her father, Samuel, was also a horse-keeper. George and Jane had two children, Jane Susan and George Frederick. At the outbreak of the First World War, George (senior) joined the Army Service Corps. Sadly, after being seriously wounded, George lost his life just hours before the end of the war, on Saturday 9th November 1918, aged 35 years. Corporal George Frederick Willis, 4th Company, 31st Division, Train. Army Service Corps, was buried in the Terlincthun British Cemetery.

William worked as a French polisher, but after a severe illness at the age of 24, he died with his mother Alice by his side. The death certificate states that he died of 'Phthisis about a year. Exhaustion'. I understand that this is Tuberculosis.

Albert Edward Willis

Bill, Iris and Bert (left to right)

Albert, my Grandfather, worked at the railway, first as a porter and then a clerk. He married Jane Yardley, my Grandmother, in Battersea in 1915. They had three children: Albert Edward, after his father (Bert to most, but Alb to his parents, brother and sister), Samuel William (Bill) and Iris May.

I remember my grandmother, Jane, as a gentle soul, but easily worried and anxious. When all three of her children enlisted for the services during World War II, she had a particularly hard time. My grandfather, Albert, was quite a stern man and would not perhaps have offered her the greatest support.

Left to right:

Samuel (Bill), Albert (Bert, my father), their mother Jane Willis (nee Yardley) and Iris.

Gert also went into service, as a domestic housemaid, but continued to live at home with her parents. She married William John Beare, in 1921, and three years later had a son, John William.

The wedding of Gertrude Willis and William Beare, 1921.

Far left, at the front is my father, Albert.

Alice Willis (nee Gardner) is seated to the right of the picture

Gert, had always been more delicate and susceptible to ill-health, and the birth seemed to take its toll. Whether due to difficulties with the birth, or not, John was born with learning difficulties and wore thick-lensed glasses from a young age. His Aunt Maude, herself described as 'incapacitated' lived with Gert and William at 46, Buckhurst Street, Bethnal Green. She took a part in John's care. Both of his parents died when he was still a teenage boy, William in 1940, and his wife Gert two years later, aged 50. John remained with his Aunt at the family home. For all his difficulties, John was the most generous soul and could see no bad in anyone. This left him vulnerable to the greed and bad intentions of others, who would take his money, and taunt him for his differences of manner. My father, John's cousin, and mother took a huge part in his care in the last decades of his life.

Maude (left) and Gert with John Beare

Albert Edward Willis

My father then, Albert Edward Willis (Bert), was the first-born son of Albert Edward Willis and Jane (nee Yardley), born in the summer of 1916. His brother and sister, Bill and Iris, followed at roughly two-year intervals. As he went through school, it was clear that he was a talented scholar, excelling in subjects both academic and artistic. One of his school exercise books still exists and demonstrates his early scientific, literary and design skills. One sadness however, was that no matter how exceptional his achievements, he never seemed able to merit the praise of his father. This obviously caused him a great deal of anguish, for it was something he occasionally mentioned, even in his old age.

Bert's pen sketches, aged 14

In his free time, he took informal lessons with a blind organist at the local church, who encouraged his love of music and taught him the rudiments of playing a keyboard instrument. This was a skill he enjoyed for the rest of his life. As an adult, his knowledge of classical music led to him not only being able to identify the composer of just about any piece of music, but also the name of the piece, its key and Opus number. He would even hazard a guess at the name of the orchestra playing the music!

Albert Edward (Bert) Willis
Taken at Iris's Wedding

Albert and Jane were able to manage on his railway clerk's income, but there was no opportunity for their children to enter university. When Bert left school, he followed a career in electrical engineering. It seemed that every opportunity for learning though, was totally utilised. His time in the drawing office honed his presentation skills and saw a change in his handwriting to the precise and beautiful print that everyone that knew him easily recognised as his. Before long he was a fully qualified electrical engineer, but at the age of 23, World War 2 began. Bert was quick to enlist with the Royal Engineers.

Iris May Willis

Bert's sister Iris was another able scholar. She also shared a love of classical music. As a girl, she would have had even less hope of attending higher education. At 19 years, she too signed up, but with the Women's' Air Force. Iris's quick reasoning and intellect were no doubt recognised as she was based at Bletchley Park, the code-breaking facility at Milton Keynes.

Samuel William (Bill) Willis

Bill was 21 years old at the outbreak of the war. He did not have the same academic record as his siblings; it must have been a hard act to follow! Bill joined the 8th Army.

This was the most difficult time for their mother, Jane. Along with thousands of other mothers, she was desperately worried about her three children. Communication was limited and she clung to any news that was received. At one point a kindly woman wrote to her from Africa, the woman had provided a meal for Bert and an army colleague. She had taken the address and was carrying out a promise she had made to the young army officers, to let their mothers know they were safe. She sent a card and inside a pressed flower from the area. It meant so much to Jane that these items are still kept safely, some 80 years after they were first sent. Living in the heart of London, reminders of the war were constant and their own lives were far from safe. Jane had always been of a rather fragile disposition and her mental health suffered.

Jane Willis (nee Yardley)

Bert's army career saw him working alongside the Royal Air Force, in Malta. He was subsequently based in North Africa and the Middle East. It seems that he was able to take a brief, five-day, respite during his time in the Middle East, and he took the opportunity to travel to Jerusalem. He visited the Church of the Holy Sepulchre and other places of Biblical interest, for which he was given a letter acknowledging the completion of his pilgrimage.

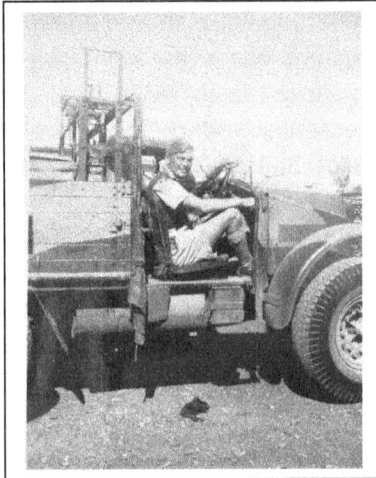

He learned to drive in the army. There were no lessons, just an order to 'Move that truck'. It did mean, however, that he was given a licence at the end of the war, no tests needed! He was 92 when he finally gave up driving.

In later years, he spoke little about his time in the army, but I remember every now and then a report broadcast on television would trigger a memory, and we'd hear the simple words, 'I've been there'. He was part of D-Day 3; this was the third day of landings, which took him to France, Belgium and Germany.

Albert Edward Willis
Royal Engineers

An experience that must had been etched in his memory for the obscene inhumanity that he witnessed, was to take place at the end of the war. He was one of the first to enter the Bergen-Belson concentration camp after it was liberated by the British 11th Armoured Division. The Royal Engineers were tasked to install power, primarily to pump desperately needed water into the camp, for the thousands who had been incarcerated there and those doing all they could to save them. This then was one of the last of his war time actions.

The family were fortunate that all, except my father's Uncle George, returned home at the end of the war. Bert resumed work as an electrical engineer, with the London Electricity Board and joined the associated cricket team at Raynes Park in South London. That was where he met Elaine Frankland, some eighteen years his junior, at one of the dances held at the pavilion. Elaine's friend Anne befriended Ron, Bert's good friend (and later, best man), and meetings became a regular occurrence.

Cricket Team
Raynes Park
c.1953

Within a year Bert and Elaine were married and settled in Morden, Surrey. This is where their three daughters were raised.

Elaine Frankland and Bert Willis

Bert could turn his hand to anything, from plumbing to woodwork, decorating to car mechanics. Every task had to be completed with the utmost precision, no imperfections in his work would be tolerated, so time would be taken to ensure absolute accuracy. His generosity of spirit and seemingly endless list of skills were soon well known by the neighbours in the little cul-de-sac. This led to a great deal of time spent in other people's lofts carrying out all manner of maintenance jobs, which he did freely and without hesitation, even though it sometimes held up the things he had planned to be doing at home.

His general knowledge would always astound as he so readily absorbed information. He was, however, generally a quiet man, not given to trivial conversation and preferring the sound of classical music. This inner peace, however, would quickly change if agitated by the unjust or foolhardy actions of others. He was most certainly not a man to withhold his views on these matters. Bert always stood up for his family, who were never in doubt of how much he cared and how proud he was of their small achievements. In a conversation with him, towards the end of his life, he said that in his role as father to us, he had always tried to be the opposite to his own father. He was certainly the best of dads to us. He died just four weeks from his 97th birthday.

Richard
GARDNER

Robert
TAYLOR

Elizabeth
EVANS

1778 - 1821
Frances
Ann
TAYLOR

1778
Richard
GARDNER

m. St Pancras, London 1802

1812
Charlotte
Susannah
CUTTELL

1804
Richard
GARDNER

1806
Frances
GARDNER

1809
William
Frederick
GARDNER

1812
Elizabeth
GARDNER

m. St Pancras, London 1833

1848
George
Frederick
WILLIS

1834
John
GARDNER

1836
Elizabeth
GARDNER

1840
George
GARDNER

1842
Caroline
GARDNER

1844
Alfred
GARDNER

1846
Alice
Maude
GARDNER

m. Camden Tn, London 1878

1882
Alice
Maud
WILLIS

1883 - 1918
George
Frederick
WILLIS

1887 - 1911
William
A
WILLIS

1890 - 1968
Albert
Edward
WILLIS

1892 - 1942
Mariam
Gertrude
WILLIS

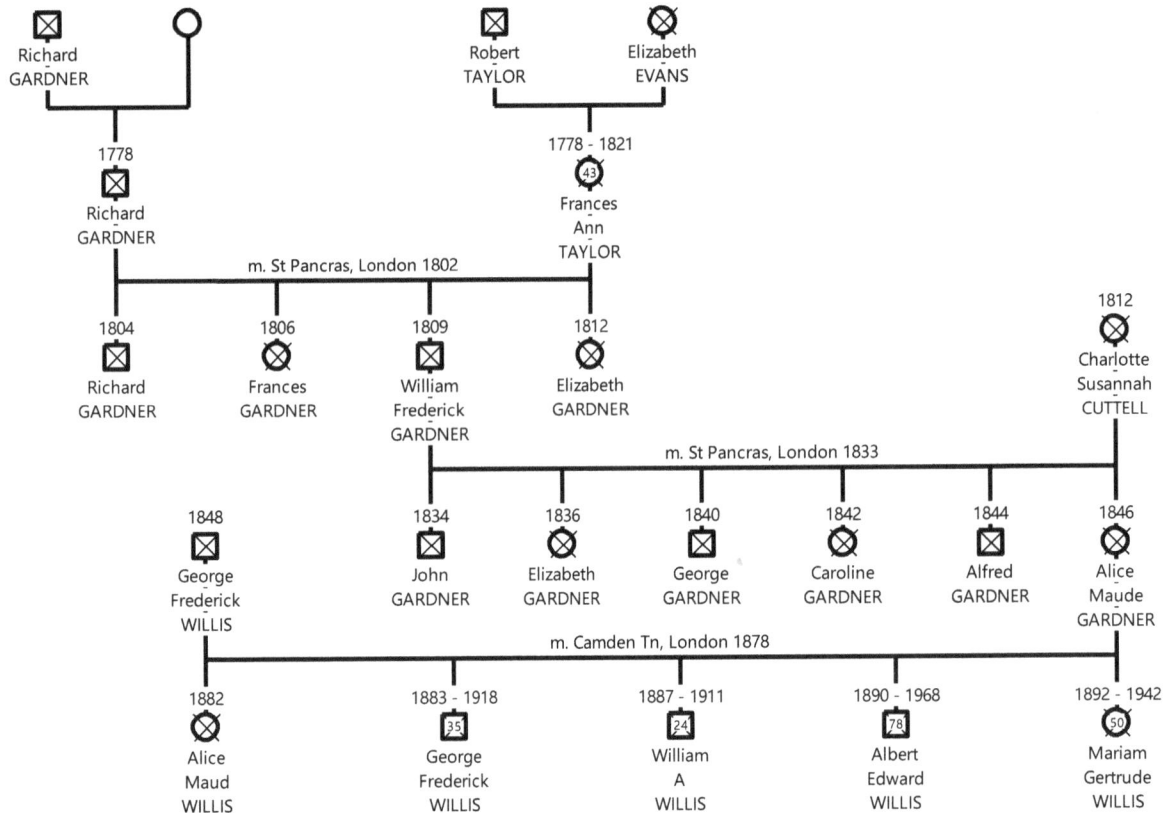

The Gardners were born and bred in the heart of London. The earliest of our direct ancestors, found so far, is Richard Gardner, who was born in around 1750, father of Richard born in 1777. Richard (junior) married Frances Ann Taylor, in the St Pancras area. Their four children were Richard, Frances, William and Elizabeth.

It is with William that information is a little more forth-coming. He was born in 1809, and at the age of eleven his mother died. His elder sister Frances, aged fourteen would quickly have taken the roll of house-keeper, with a considerable responsibility for the care of their sister Elizabeth, aged eight. William started to work as a baker journeyman (journeyman meaning he was paid by the day, rather than being employed on a regular salary), eventually making this his career.

Like his father Richard, William met a local woman and married at the Parish Church of St Pancras. This however, would have been a different church, due to major changes in the intervening years.

The parish of St Pancras had once stretched all the way from Highgate to Oxford Street. By the early 1800s the original church had become severely neglected. Changes in the population also meant that fewer lived near to the church whilst the southern part of the parish had grown rapidly. A church was needed for those living in the newly built up areas surrounding Euston Square.

A competition was held, resulting in thirty or more submissions of possible designs for the new church, resulting in acceptance of the design by a local architect William Inwood. Isaac Seabrook was the builder.

Building work started in 1819, with the first stone laid by the Duke of York at a special ceremony. The stone was carved with a Greek inscription, reflecting the style of the design. The English translation is, "May the light of the blessed Gospel thus ever illuminate the dark temples of the Heathen."

The church was completed and consecrated by the Bishop of London, in 1822. It could seat 2,500 people. It is now Grade 1 listed, by English Heritage, due to it being a significant early example of Greek Revival architecture, greatly influenced by the design of the Acropolis, in Athens.

To the west end of the church are Ionic style pillars and at the centre is a domed vestibule. Its most celebrated features, however, are two sets of caryatids that stand above the north and south entrances to the Crypt. Each holds an extinguished torch or an empty jug, said to reflect their position as guardians of the deceased.

So, William married his bride, Charlotte Cuttell, in 1833, at the new St Pancras Church. They set up home in the St Giles in the Field area of London, where they had John, Elizabeth and George. William continued his trade as a baker and towards the end of 1840, they moved to 30, Clarence Gardens, St Pancras.

Clarence Gardens, St Pancras

Clarence Gardens, had been planned as a second market for the area, but was finally developed into a residential square. Being of rectangular proportions it had a large central garden. Osnaburgh Street divided the square into two gardens. The houses surrounding it, which became derelict, have now been replaced by low rise flats. The original terraces of three stories, were described at the time as unpretentious, built of red brick, with a plastered 'rusticated facing' to the ground floor level. It was intended to use the first floor as the main living area, as it had larger sash windows than those above or below. The houses to the east had semi-circular-headed windows and doors, whereas those on the west had horizontal heads. Some of the houses in the centre, both east and west, had additional fancy architraves and balconies. The houses were leased from 1824, so would have been about fifteen years old when William and Charlotte first took on their lease.

It was here that Caroline, Alfred and Alice were born. As was typical of the time, the children went to school until the age of eleven. This would have meant that most schools were what we now consider to be primary phase schools. John Gardner, secured an apprenticeship with a local cabinet-maker. Elizabeth, found work as a dressmaker, probably working from home. George, at the age of eleven, was an errand boy (a much-needed service before telephones came into everyday use). At 21, he was a printer, as was his younger brother Alfred. At 19, Caroline was a flower-maker.

Following the various marriages of their children, William and Charlotte moved the short distance to 53, Queen Street. This was a house with multiple occupancy. In 1871, the couple were sharing the small home with two lodgers, a mother and daughter. At the time of their daughter Alice's marriage to George Willis, in 1876, the young couple's marriage certificate states that they were staying at the same address. In the intervening years, I believe that Alice went into service as a housemaid, but as yet I have no records of this.

The Yardleys and Toyes

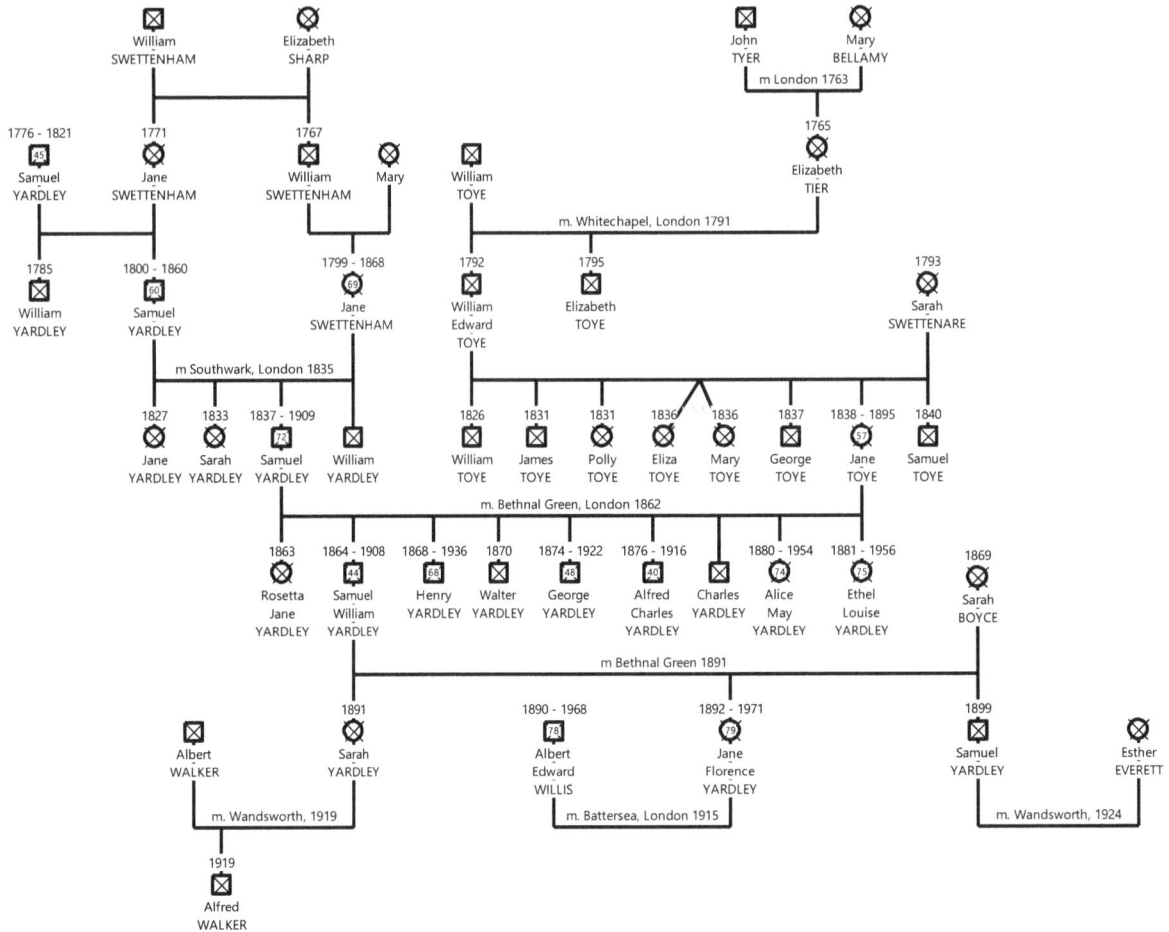

William SWETTENHAM — Elizabeth SHARP

John TYER — Mary BELLAMY
m London 1763

1776 - 1821 (45) Samuel YARDLEY — 1771 Jane SWETTENHAM

1767 William SWETTENHAM — Mary

William TOYE — 1765 Elizabeth TIER
m. Whitechapel, London 1791

1785 William YARDLEY

1800 - 1860 (58) Samuel YARDLEY — 1799 - 1868 (69) Jane SWETTENHAM
m Southwark, London 1835

1792 William Edward TOYE

1795 Elizabeth TOYE

1793 Sarah SWETTENARE

1827 Jane YARDLEY | 1833 Sarah YARDLEY | 1837 - 1909 (72) Samuel YARDLEY | William YARDLEY

1826 William TOYE | 1831 James TOYE | 1831 Polly TOYE | 1836 Eliza TOYE | 1836 Mary TOYE | 1837 George TOYE | 1838 - 1895 (57) Jane TOYE | 1840 Samuel TOYE

m. Bethnal Green, London 1862

1863 Rosetta Jane YARDLEY | 1864 - 1908 (44) Samuel William YARDLEY | 1868 - 1936 (68) Henry YARDLEY | 1870 Walter YARDLEY | 1874 - 1922 (48) George YARDLEY | 1876 - 1916 (40) Alfred Charles YARDLEY | Charles YARDLEY | 1880 - 1954 (74) Alice May YARDLEY | 1881 - 1956 (75) Ethel Louise YARDLEY

1869 Sarah BOYCE
m Bethnal Green 1891

Albert WALKER | 1891 Sarah YARDLEY

1890 - 1968 (78) Albert Edward WILLIS | 1892 - 1971 (79) Jane Florence YARDLEY
m. Battersea, London 1915

1899 Samuel YARDLEY | Esther EVERETT
m. Wandsworth, 1924

m. Wandsworth, 1919

1919 Alfred WALKER

As true 'EastEnders', London was home to the Yardleys from at least the mid 1700s, when my 4xG Grandfather Samuel was born. His son Samuel, was born in Bethnal Green in 1801, and married Jane Swettenham in Southwark, in 1835. The names Samuel and Jane then featured in the family for the next three generations. Samuel was a licenced victualler (inn-keeper or publican), a trade that would also recur within the family. He ran the 'Old Pitts Head' 17, Tyssen Street, Bethnal Green, from around 1835, and that is where his children Jane, Sarah, Samuel and William grew up.

At the same time, William Yardley, Samuel's brother, was also a publican, running the 'Half Moon and Crown' public house, 37, Bacon Street. William's wife Mary, and children William and Joseph, also experienced life growing up in a pub.

It cannot have been an easy life. Bethnal Green had seen huge growth in its population since the mid-1700s and by 1800, numbers had risen to around 22,000, making its population as large as Oxford and Cambridge combined. The area, once a thriving centre for the weaving industry, had gone through a period of closures and massive reductions in the work force. Many were finding it hard to feed and clothe themselves and the housing stock had fallen into disrepair leading to serious deprivation and squalor. The Yardleys had, at least, a roof over their heads and an income, but it must have been a difficult existence with a young family. Pubs could be places of over-indulgence and no doubt a draw for 'women of the night', a growing occupation given the desperation of the circumstances of many among Bethnal Green's large population.

Samuel Yardley was the publican of the 'Cooper's Arms', 12, James Street, Bethnal Green, for a time, before relinquishing it to his nephew William, in 1851. He then took over the 'Buck's Head', 26, Chilton Street, just a short distance away, once again moving the family. When Samuel died, in 1860, his wife Jane took over the running of the pub, with their son Samuel working alongside her as barman. In 1861, aged 25, Samuel took the pub over from his mother. He was married the following year and his new wife, Jane Toye, moved into the pub. The Toyes were another East End family, but Jane's family background had been linked to weaving, mat-making and sash-making. She came from a large family of eight children. There appears to be a good chance that Samuel had known Jane since early childhood. Her grandmother had lived in Tyssen Street, where Samuel had lived until he was about seven years old. Jane was just a year younger than him.

Samuel and Jane went on to have a large family themselves, nine children in all: six boys and three girls. They were: Rosetta, Samuel (known by his middle name, William), Henry, Walter, Arthur, George, Alfred, Alice and finally Ethel. The pub must have been doing reasonably well, as in 1881, they had a nursemaid/domestic and a general servant, help that I imagine was much needed both with the cleaning of the pub and the care of the children.

William, Walter and Alfred all followed the family into the pub trade. Henry though, became a butcher, Arthur, a lithographic printer, and George was a chair frame and cabinet maker.

For a while, William tried other occupations. In 1891, he was a line worker on the railway, and for a short while he was recorded as a plumber. By this time, he had met and married a local woman, Sarah Boyce and the couple had had their first baby girl, Sarah. They had two further children: Jane Florence (my Grandmother), and Samuel. In 1901, William went back into the pub trade and took over the 'Old Pitts Head' in Brick Lane. Although the same name as his grandfather's pub, it was a short distance away, in Shoreditch.

William's father, Samuel, continued to run the 'Buck's Head', with his brother Walter helping as barman. Walter married Alice Winston, in 1901. Tragically, both Alice and his father Samuel, died in 1909. This must have been an immensely difficult time for Walter. The pub was taken over by younger brother Alfred, with brother Arthur, and sisters Alice and Ethel all unmarried and still living in their childhood home. Walter, who had, at some point started to work as a hawker (or peddler) ended up in the Bethnal Green Workhouse. Hopefully, only a temporary admission while he pieced his life back together.

Of William's three children, only Sarah continued in the beer retailing trade. She married Albert Walker in 1919 and took over 'The Old Farm House' pub, at 40, Doddington Road, Battersea. My mother recalls Sarah as an exuberant, friendly woman, who would have made her customers feel welcomed and comfortable.

William's middle daughter, Jane, was very different to her sister. Timid and disliking large groups or unfamiliar situations, she would have been ill-at-ease in public houses, despite her upbringing. Jane married Albert Willis, in 1915, and they too settled in Battersea. Jane took pleasure in her three children, but her own struggles with large social gatherings even prevented her from attending their subsequent marriages.

Samuel, William's youngest child, worked as a member of the technical staff for the People's Dispensary for Sick Animals (PDSA). He married Esther Everett, in 1924, and settled in the Southgate area of London.

George
BOWLES — Sarah

| 1798 | 1799 | 1818 | 1805 |
| Charles BOYCE | Elizabeth | Isaac BOWLES | Eleanor |

| 1833 | 1838 | 1840 | 1842 | 1835 | 1843 | 1842 |
| Jane BOYCE | George BOYCE | James BOYCE | Thomas BOYCE | Maria Ann BOWLES | Emma BOWLES | Eleanor BOWLES |

| 1864 - 1908 | 1864 | 1869 | 1871 | 1875 | 1877 | 1879 | 1880 | 1884 |
| Samuel William YARDLEY | Eleanor BOYCE | Sarah BOYCE | Maria BOYCE | Mary BOYCE | Hannah BOYCE | Robert BOYCE | Thomas BOYCE | William BOYCE |

m. Bethnal Green, 1891

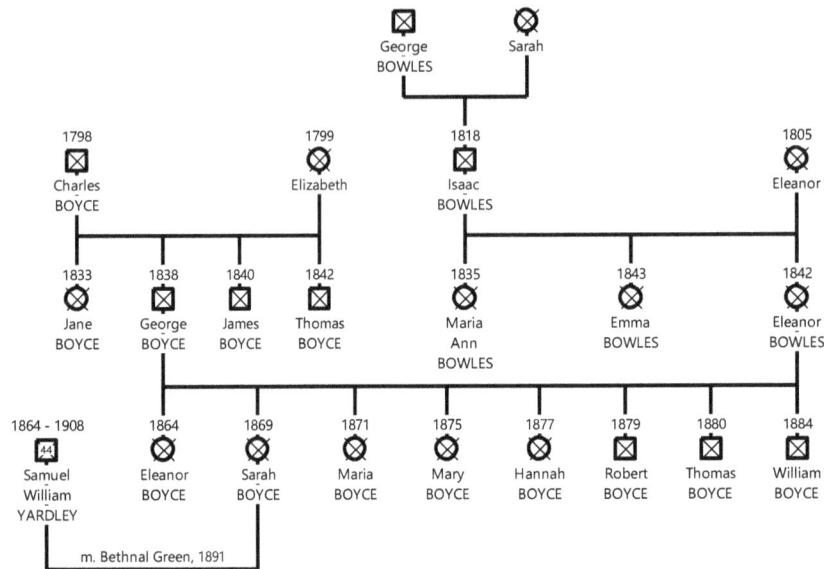

As with many families living in the Spitalfields area of London, that is the area that includes Shoreditch, Bethnal Green and Whitechapel, the early Boyces were silk weavers. Silk weaving had grown significantly in the area in the late 17th century, when around 70,000 Protestant Huguenots came from France in order to escape religious persecution under King Louis XIV of France. They brought with them little except their weaving skills. The Edict of Nantes had been revoked in 1695, making the Huguenot Protestants' worship illegal and unacceptable in France. Under public pressure, and with forecasted benefits to the economy, King Charles II allowed Protestant refugees to enter England with their goods free of duty.

The Huguenots were skilled weavers of tapestries, hangings and fabrics, and the East End became a centre for weaving and crafts. By 1831, around 20,000 looms were operated in domestic homes, rather than in dedicated workshops. Due to this, they left little mark on the London architecture. Their presence can, however, be seen in some of the large East End houses, built in the 17th and 18th centuries for the weavers and silk merchants, which have larger windows. This allowed the weavers to work later into the night.

Charles Boyce and his wife Elizabeth were both silk weavers and their daughter Jane and son James followed them in this work. Their eldest son George, however, set himself up as a general dealer in Bethnal Green.

George met Eleanor Bowles, a young woman from Whitechapel. Eleanor's father was a tinman and later a carver and guilder. They married in 1864 and went on to have eight children, five daughters followed by three sons. Tragically, George died aged 42, around the time of his youngest son William's birth. It must have been a dreadful blow for Eleanor and her young family. However, she proved to be a resourceful woman, managing to maintain the family in their home in Granby Street, by using her skills in needlework.

Two sons, Thomas and William, became tailors. Robert chose a career in wood-turning. Until marriage, daughters Eleanor, Sarah, Maria, Mary and Hannah were employed variously as cap-maker, needle-worker, confectionary shop assistant and chemist's assistant. No doubt, while living at home, their income would have been a welcome contribution towards the household bills.

Sarah, my Great Grandmother, met and married Samuel Yardley, in 1891.

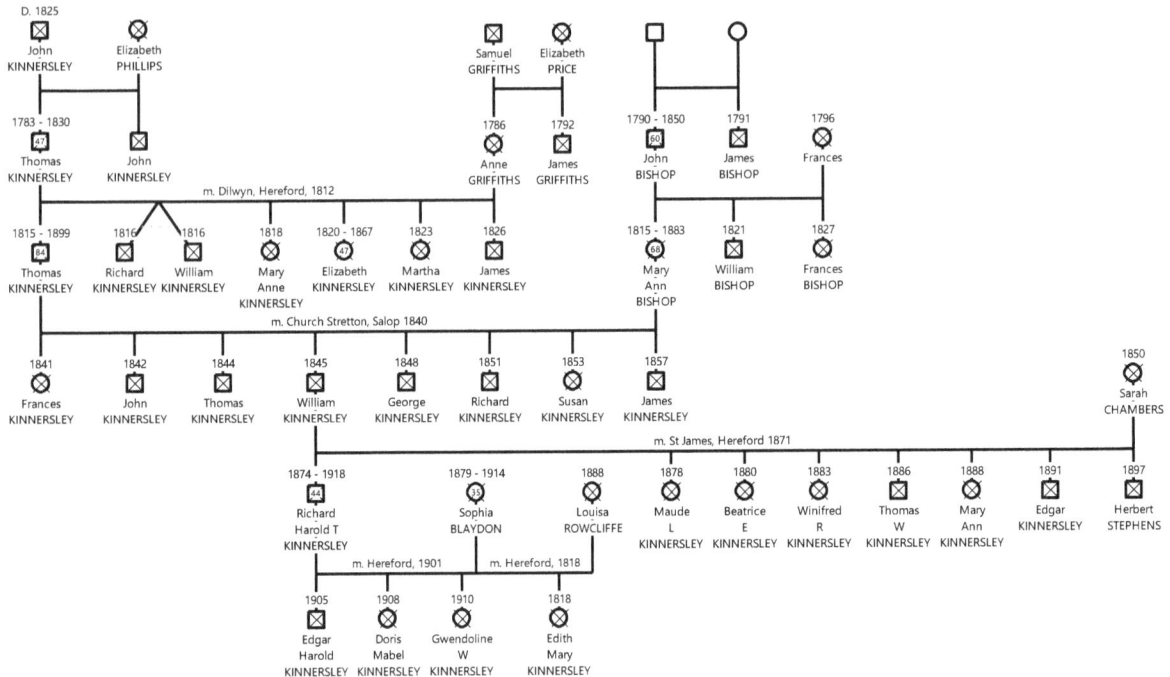

The surname Kinnersley (and place-name) is based upon the Old English first name 'Cynheard', with the Old English word 'leah', meaning 'forest clearing', as a suffix. The place-name as a whole meant 'forest clearing belonging to Cynheard'. The ancient Kinnersley family first appears in Herefordshire, residing at Kinnersley Castle, this was before the Norman Conquest, in 1066. When the 'Great Survey' was conducted on the command of William the Conqueror, in 1086, John de Kynnardsley, a knight, was living at and owned Kynnardsley Castle, in Hereford. The old gentleman was blind and living with him were twelve sons.

Kinnersley Castle, Herefordshire

Around 160 years later, Hugo de Kynnardsleye, a soldier of the Cross, accompanied Prince Edward to the Holy Land. He was knighted and was Sheriff of Herefordshire in 1249-1250. It was some twenty years later, c1270, that he again accompanied Prince Edward in a Crusade to the Holy Land. It was not until 1274 that they returned to England. By then Edward had been King of England (Edward I) for nearly 15 months, his father, King Henry III having died in 1272. By then Hugo de Kynnardsleye had already been knighted and had added Jerusalem crosses to the Arms.

The earliest Kinnersley, that I have found as a direct ancestor is John, married to Elizabeth Phillips. They lived in Dilwyn, Hereford, six miles from the village of Kinnersley. Their son Thomas Kinnersley, Bill's 3xG Grandfather, was born in 1785. He was owner of a significant area of land and called himself a 'Yeoman'. Thomas married Anne Griffiths in 1812 and they had seven children, including twin boys. The recurring boys' names in our Kinnersley family are John, Thomas, William and Richard. There is not such a clear pattern amongst the girl's names. The couple married in Dilwyn, but at some point, moved to Preston Wynne, about fifteen miles west, which is where Thomas acquired his land holding. When he died in 1830, aged 47, his brother John was farmer of the land. This, he continued to do, while the estate was held by Thomas's executors. His son and heir, another Thomas, born in 1815, was still a minor.

Thomas (junior) married Mary Ann Bishop, a young woman from across the border, in Shropshire. Mary Ann's father, John, also called himself 'Yeoman'. He was the owner of Sibdon Castle, where the family lived. Thomas and Mary Ann married at St Michael's Church, in the castle grounds.

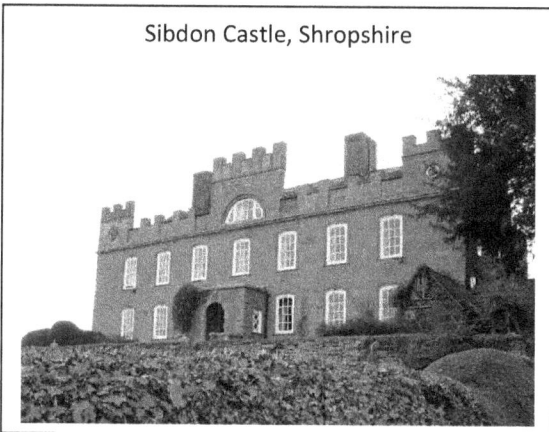
Sibdon Castle, Shropshire

Sibdon Castle, was built on the site of an earlier medieval fortification or manor house, Shepeton Corbet. The current Sibdon Castle is not a castle, but an early 17th century stone country house, built by the Corbet family. It was modernised in the 18th century and battlements added, making it 'castellated' in around 1800. There is a courtyard and stone stable block to the rear of the property.

St Michael's Church

On the estate is a small hamlet, where St Michael's Church stands. The church was built around 1180, with additions over time. The church, a lodge (on the estate) and Sibdon Castle are now all Grade II listed. Within the hamlet are also a farm, a small number of cottages and numerous outbuildings. To the north-east lies Sibdon Pool, a 1.3 hectare lake. A private tree-lined avenue or carriage driveway connects the hamlet with Clun Road. Today, a number of public footpaths or rights of way cross through the hamlet, giving access to the church and the 'Shropshire Way'.

Thomas and Mary Ann settled in Withington, Hereford. A year after their marriage, the 1841 Census shows them with a baby daughter, Frances, after Mary Ann's mother. Living with them, or perhaps visiting, is Thomas's sister Mary Ann. There are also two female servants and a fifteen-year-old agricultural labourer. Life seemed to be going well for the young family. They moved back to Shropshire the following year, and it was there, in Clunbury, that sons John, Thomas and William were born.

Thomas seems to have been of strong physique. He was not afraid of voicing his opinions and showed strength of character, admired by his friends, as the following excerpt from a local newspaper demonstrates:

'Amateur Reaping – A correspondent sends us the following:-

"On the 22nd Aug., being Ludlow fair-day, a party of gentlemen met at the Elephant and Castle Commercial Inn to regale themselves. During the evening the conversation was chiefly on the harvest, and finally on the propriety of mowing wheat – a practice resorted to in the greatest part of that neighbourhood. Mr T. Kinnersley of Clunton, son of the late T. Kinnersley, Esq. of Preston Wynne, near Hereford, remarked the inutility of mowing wheat when men were to be found that could cut with the broad hook an acre per day, which gave rise to the question, "Who can?" Mr Kinnersley replied, "I can." Some of the party being incredulous as to the feat being performed, a wager was laid between Mr Kinnersley and Mr Tait of the Bach, which amounted to a considerable sum. Mr Kinnersley was backed by E. Downes, Esq., Brooms; W. Blockley, Esq., Broadstone; R. Carter, Esq., Ashford, &c. On Mr Tait's side were John Bishop, Esq., Sibdon Castle; Mr M. Evans, landlord of the inn, &c. The feat was to be performed on the Wednesday following. Mr T. Langslow of Abcott-hall, who was present, with his wonted good nature kindly gave permission for an acre of wheat in his field to become the scene of action. Mr K. was allowed from five o'clock a.m. until eight o'clock p.m. E. Dawes, Esq., New-house, who measured the ground, was chosen as referee, and A. Woolley, Esq., Abcott, umpire. The wheat stood well, though a strong crop. The amateur reaper, undaunted, entered the field, and, as the village clock struck five, he commenced his laborious undertaking, and nobly won his wager in 13½ hours, being an hour and a half under the limited time, apparently without fatigue, and was loudly cheered by his friends and supporters.'

-Salopian Journal, September 1842-

So, Thomas won the wager, and his father-in-law John Bishop had to pay the 'considerable sum'.

Lane Head Farm, Eaton Bishop, Herefordshire

Another move, around 1845, took Thomas and Mary Ann back to Hereford. The couple became tenant farmers at Lane Head Farm, where Thomas farmed 300 acres of land. This was where sons George and Richard were born.

It is unclear whether a major event befell the family or just a gradual decline in the farm's viability, but Thomas and Mary left the farm in 1851. A newspaper advertisement announced the sale by auction of:

> 'Farming Stock of CATTLE, HORSES, PIGS, IMPLEMENTS, Hay, Clover and Straw, Swedish Turnips, Mangel Worzel, HOUSEHOLD FURNITURE and other Effects, the property of Mr Thomas Kinnersley who is leaving the estate.'

The advertisement goes on to give details of the livestock and implements:

> 'TWO FAT COWS, one cow and calf, two three-years-old heifers in calf, six two-years-old ditto, four two-years-old bullocks, a very well bred two-years-old bull, and 12 yearlings.
>
> HORSE STOCK: One cart gelding, five ditto mares (three of which are in foal, all young, sound and excellent workers), bay nag horse (five years old, good in harness), grey pony in foal, brown cart gelding rising two, grey ditto filly, two weaned colts and a three-years-old mute under duty and remarkably active.
>
> PIGS: Three sows with pigs, one boar pig and nine strong stores.
>
> IMPLEMENTS: Three broad wheel waggons, (one equal to new, with double and single shafts, high boards and all requisite fittings), three broad wheel carts, iron G.O., double and single wheel, and other ploughs, two pairs breast harrows, one horse patent (by Saunders and Williams), two horse ditto (by Ditto), five-horses-power threshing-machine with chaff engine attached and carriage belonging, 4-horse land scuffler, turnip ditto, turnip engine, roll, three-furrow drill, winnowing machine, blower, try, piling-iron, and other small implements; about six dozen hurdles, G.O., long, and short gearing, gig and harness; rick of peas, two ditto of clover, part of a rick of hay, and a quantity of wheat and barley straw, with the use of folds, and c., to the 1st of May next, also a quantity of swedes and mangel worzel; one 500 gallon and ten hogshead casks, tubs, and c.
>
> DAIRY: One pair milk leads (five feet by three), meat safe, large flour bin, two stone cheese-presses, barrel churn, vats, milk pail and other small articles.'

From this list, it seems that Thomas was engaged in mixed farming, he kept livestock, grew some vegetable crops (probably mainly as animal fodder – mangel worzel being a root vegetable grown mainly for that purpose), had dairy cows and probably had an orchard for the production of cider.

The advertisement goes on to list the furniture being auctioned:

> 'THE HOUSEHOLD FURNITURE comprises four-post, tent, and stump bedsteads, feather beds, blankets, and bed-linen, eight day clock, oak bureau, sofa, mahogany sideboard, square, round, and other tables in oak or mahogany, chairs, dressing-tables and chamber appointments.'

It would appear that all but personal items, were sold.

Thomas and Mary were housed at the Coningsby Hospital Alms houses, in Hereford. Eligibility, possibly due to them being members of the Hereford Salvation Army, combined with their having fallen on hard times. It was there, shortly after the move, that Mary Ann gave birth to their daughter Susan, and Thomas started to work as a butcher. Four years later, their final son, James, was born.

Conningsby Hospital Almshouses

Conningsby Alms Houses Courtyard

The house was small and in need of renovation, having been built for ex-servicemen and marines in 1614, with little in the way of maintenance over the years. Six dwellings surrounded a courtyard with a water pump in the centre. Each home had one upstairs and one downstairs room as well as access to a communal space and chapel.

Conningsby Chapel

George followed his father and became a butcher. As a sixteen-year-old, still living at home, he almost cost the family their lives. One night, in February 1863, he returned from market and went to bed, leaving a candle burning. The candle ignited a wooden partition, which was soon in flames. According to the 'Hereford Journal' it was Mary Ann who discovered the fire and raised the alarm. A number of neighbours helped to put out the fire, which George had slept through, unaware of the chaos he had unwittingly caused. Fortunately, no-one was seriously hurt and the £5 damages was covered by Thomas's insurance.

Hard as they worked, it seems that Thomas and Mary Ann could not escape the debts that had preceded their move to the alms house. In July, just five months after the fire, Thomas was declared bankrupt at a Birmingham court.

As the children became old enough to work, they moved into lodgings and therefore to independent lives. George and his wife moved to nearby Edgar Street, where he could continue to work with his father. William moved out of the family home and boarded with a police constable and his family, meanwhile he took up work as a printer compositor.

Kinnersley Butcher's Shop

Eventually, Thomas and Mary were in a position to move out of the alms house and took over a shop at 79, Widemarsh Street, close to Widemarsh Gate, which they set up as their butcher's shop and home.

The shop is the one on the left. It has a large shop window and door on the side of the building, today used for access to upper floor flats. Without the side hedge, the window would have been in full view from the main town area.

Thomas continued as a butcher and was keen to fulfil his role in society. Each Christmas, no doubt with the help of George, he entered into the street festivities, producing extra meat for a special window display.

On one occasion he visited the cemetery at Preston Wynne, with two of his children (who had made the trip from London). Thomas found that the fence had been broken and the cemetery was severely overgrown. He was quick to write to the editor of the local newspaper, eloquently expressing his anguish at the sight, and offering to help raise funds and organise the repair.

To the Editor of the Hereford Times.

Sir, - It is soothing to one's mind to see the graves of those who have departed this life neatly and reverently trimmed and kept in good order as they are at our cemeteries and in many of our churchyards, being familiar with which state of things the contrast is all the more distressing to one's feelings. But I will come at once to the secret of my discontent. Last Sunday, as two of my children had come down from London on a visit, I drove them over to Preston Wynne churchyard to see the graves of a brother and sister of theirs and the graves of my father and mother.

I have known this little "God's acre" ever since I can remember, kept tidily with a good fence round it to keep out stock. I can't, sir, express the pain I felt to see what a state the churchyard is now in. The fence is broken down, or was on Sunday, and stock could get in when they liked, while the grass is as high as the top of the tombstones except where it had been trod and "wozzled" down by the sheep and other animals, whose droppings were about the graves. I found on asking a passer-by that the animals had been driven out not quite an hour before, and it was near time for service. I will confess that I was so pained that I wept at the sight of the neglect I saw. Can anyone tell me who is responsible for the proper maintenance of the fence and the grounds and the keeping of them in respectable order? If no one is responsible, I am quite willing to head a subscription for the erection of a new fence and the putting of the ground in proper order.

THOMAS KINNERSLEY

79, Widemarsh Street, Hereford, September 26th, 1882.

We visited the Holy Trinity Church, at Preston Wynne, in search of the graves. The church is set in the middle of a field (once owned by Thomas Kinnersley (senior)). There is no road or drive leading to the church, instead it is accessed via a kissing gate from a lane and then across the farmer's land. A finger sign shows that the route is a public footpath, but there is no path in sight. The very kind church warden had warned us prior to our visit that the farmer dislikes people crossing his land and has been known to place a bull in the field!... We were lucky. Just sheep in our case.

Holy Trinity Church, Preston Wynne

Unfortunately, the graves are no longer visible, but it was good to stand in the place once frequented by our ancestors.

Thomas's words must have had the required impact - all perimeter fences were in good repair and the grass relatively short!

Mary Ann died in 1883. We visited the Hereford Cemetery and were able to locate her grave, almost entirely covered in ivy and brambles. It was possible to clear most of the overgrowth to reveal some of the most touching words:

In Loving Memory of

MARY ANN

The beloved wife of THOMAS KINNERSLEY

Butcher of this city

Who departed this life Sept. 21st 1883

Aged 68 Years

Released at length from cares and lingering pains

Here peaceful sleep a mother's loved remains,

She lived in Jesus and in peace she died.

Her husband's joy, her children's friend and guide.

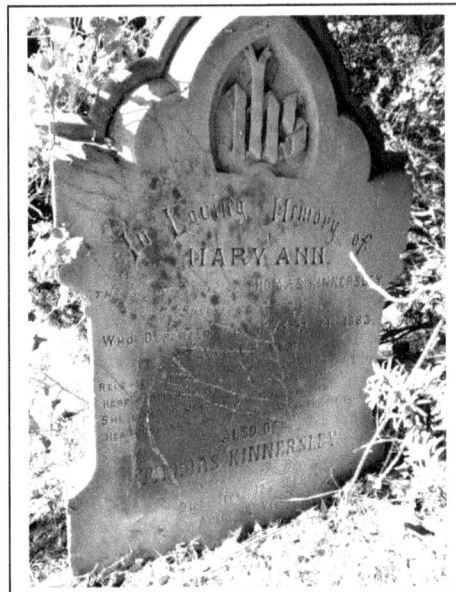

Their youngest son James remained at home with Thomas, even after his marriage and the arrival of his own baby daughter. James took over his father's work as butcher, and Thomas retired. Thomas Kinnersley died in 1899, aged 84 years. The Hereford Journal, at the time, gave a vivid portrait of his funeral, giving a little more information about him and his life:

'Rather pretty and pathetic was the funeral of Thomas Kinnersley, an old Salvation Army member of Hereford, last Thursday. About sixty 'officers and soldiers,' men and lasses, all wearing white scarfs, assembled with their brass band outside the alms house, where the deceased was lying in his coffin. An outside service was commenced with the tune, 'Home Sweet Home,' and prayer was offered by the captain. The deceased, formerly a well-known butcher, was a tall heavy man, so he was borne in a hearse, instead of being carried by the bearers across to the Salvation Barracks. Here the service continued, and then the procession marched with slow music to the cemetery, where at the grave, the ceremony concluded with prayer, hymns, scripture and a short address.'

Thomas was laid to rest with Mary and his name added to the grave stone.

Thomas and Mary Ann's son William met and married Sarah Chambers, at the Chapel of St James, in Hereford, in 1871. They settled at number 35, Harold Street, and it was there that Richard Harold Thomas Kinnersley, Bill's Grandfather, was born. Maud, Beatrice, Winifred, Thomas, Mary and Edgar followed. The family moved to Eign Farm, in Tupsley, Hereford, during the 1880s. This was a small farm on Eign Hill, not far from the River Wye.

St James, Hereford

In 1901, the Census return shows that Sarah was on her own at Eign Farm, working as a laundress. She had with her, one son, Thomas, daughters Maud and Mary Ann, and an 'adopted son', four-year-old Herbert Stephens. William had left the family home to live in Kidderminster, Worcestershire, and he had taken his youngest son Edgar with him. He was still working as a printer compositor but was a lodger in the house of George Hardy, probably a work colleague as he was of the same profession. We cannot know for certain, but perhaps Herbert was the son of Sarah and a Mr Stephens, it would be a possible reason for the couple's separation. The 1911 Census, shows that the couple remained apart. William stayed in Kidderminster, however, his son Edgar returned to live with his mother. Herbert Stephens also remained at Eign Farm.

Richard Kinnersley married Sophia Blaydon in 1901. They had both been raised in Hereford and settled in the St Owen area. Richard had completed his apprenticeship as a tailor and continued in this profession. The couple had three children: Edgar, Doris and Gwendoline. Tragically, when Gwendoline was just four years old, her mother Sophia died. Continuing his work, while caring for his young family, must have been very difficult for Richard. In such circumstances, it may have been that one of his four sisters was able to step in to help.

Richard Harold Thomas Kinnersley

It is not clear how he met Louisa Rowcliffe, a Devonshire woman, fourteen years younger than himself. She had previously been a carer for her sick mother, so it is possible that she was involved in some way with the care of Richard's children or as housekeeper. What is apparent, is that, the couple became close and, in 1918, Louisa found herself pregnant. They married in the April and should have been looking forward to the birth of their baby, but tragedy was to strike the family again. Richard died three months later, during an influenza epidemic that swept the country. This was three months before the birth of their little daughter Edith Mary, Bill's mother.

Richard and Sophia's children, were taken in by one of their aunts. Louisa married again when her little girl, Edie, Bill's mother, was two years old.

1771
James
CHAMBERS

1781
Mary
BISHOP

Thomas
JONES

m Lyonshall, Hereford 1819

1820
Marianne
CHAMBERS

1823
Susanna
CHAMBERS

1824
Elizabeth
CHAMBERS

1825
Caroline
CHAMBERS

1828 - 1907
James
CHAMBERS

1831
Caroline
CHAMBERS

1821
Sarah
JONES

m. Presteigne, Hereford 1849

1845
William
KINNERSLEY

1850
Sarah
Ann
CHAMBERS

1854
Mary
CHAMBERS

1857
Elizabeth
CHAMBERS

m. St James, Hereford 1871

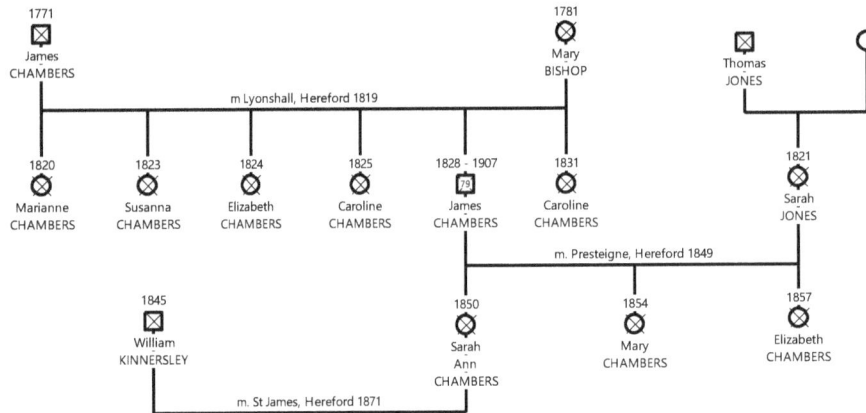

The early Chambers ancestors were also found living in Herefordshire. James Chambers, born in 1771, was an agricultural labourer. He married Mary Bishop, who was ten years his junior, in Lyonshall, Hereford. They settled in Kington and had six children, five daughters and one son. Sadly, only two of the children survived infancy: Elizabeth and James.

The young James did not follow the path trodden by his father. Instead, he set himself up as a tinman and brazier. He married Sarah, the daughter of Thomas Jones, a nail-maker. It seems likely that the metal-working commonality between the families was how the couple met.

There were four iron foundries in Herefordshire at the time. The largest was in Victoria Road, Kington. This was almost certainly the place that Thomas Jones worked. The ironmongery business had been founded at the beginning of the 18th century. A workshop and warehouse were then built at Lower Cross, followed by an ironworking site near the old Market Hall, with forges for nail making. The business prospered and in 1820 a new site, at Sunset, was developed. Large stone buildings were erected to house a foundry and workshops. A weir, built across the nearby Back Brook, diverted water to power a waterwheel, which in turn drove bellows, hammers and other machinery. Continued growth saw the erection of Nail Row, a complex including ten stone cottages and eight forges where the nail-makers were able to live and work.

Thomas Jones's daughter Sarah was working as a household servant, in Kington, until her marriage to James Chambers. The age gap between them was similar to that of James' parents, but in their case, it was Sarah who was the elder of the two, being ten years older than her husband.

The couple had three daughters: Sarah Ann, Mary and Elizabeth. They had a number of address changes, living for the most part, near to one of the most unhealthy areas of the city of Hereford, St Owen Gate. This was in close proximity to the open sewer that was the Castle Mill pond. The area was described as being in 'a most miserable condition', twelve households had just two outdoor privies between them. Disease and infection was rife and the smell must have been overwhelming.

To add to the family's troubles, in June 1864, James, suffering from mental health problems, was admitted to the 'Abergavenny Lunatic Asylum' in Monmouthshire, leaving Sarah and the girls to fend for themselves. It must, however, also have been somewhat of a relief, since his all-consuming delusions had led James to attack his wife on a number of occasions. James remained at the Asylum for nine-and-a-half months. He was not at that point regarded as ready for discharge but was 'relieved'. This meant that his care and safety were transferred to the custody of family and friends.

Unfortunately, the family were unable to cope. James was readmitted four months later. He was still delusional and given to violent outbursts. He could 'shout at the top of his voice for an hour altogether' or go for long periods without speaking, just nodding or shaking his head. One of his daughters said he never seemed to sleep, mumbling to himself through the night.

Sarah, obviously a resourceful woman, found work as a grocer. Her eldest daughter, Sarah Ann, then met William Kinnersley, a printer compositor. William was living in Harold Street, still in the same parish, but away from the poorest housing. It can only be assumed, that a dwelling became available next to William's and he may have been instrumental in helping them to attain it, for in the 1871 census William was recorded as living with his new wife Sarah Ann at 35, Harold Street. Sarah Chambers and her two remaining daughters were at number 36. The records are consecutive.

35, Harold Street

We visited Harold Street, and found only odd numbered houses on one side. The old militia barracks and parade ground (founded in 1856) taking the area on the opposite side of the street. The unaltered odd numbered houses, however, have two doors. One is obviously the front door. The other looks like a side access door and may indicate that the houses were formerly split into two dwellings with independent access. This would account for there now being no even numbered houses. So, it would seem likely that Sarah and her daughters lived above William and Sarah Ann.

When the Hereford 'Burghill Asylum' opened in 1871, James Chambers was transferred from Abergavenny. The case notes describe him as still suffering from fits of peak excitement, delusions that people (including his wife) were 'by means of various arts attempting to pass an evil influence over him to his injury'. Much of the time, however, he would remain slumped in a chair, refusing to engage with anything offered to him.

Sarah herself, was suffering from sporadic Cholera, no doubt this was a condition contracted from her previous poor living conditions. She was fortunate to have William and Sarah Ann living so close to her, who I am sure, along with daughters Mary and Elizabeth, would have been able to give her care and support as her health deteriorated. She died of heart failure caused by the Cholera she had contracted, aged 56 years, five months after Sarah Ann and William's marriage. Son-in-law William was with her. It might have been expected that Sarah would have a pauper's grave, given her struggle in life, but just as they had tried to look after her in the final chapter of her life, it seems that William and Sarah Ann took care of things after her death. She had a substantial headstone, that is still easily legible after many years.

Following her death, daughters Mary and Elizabeth both moved away from the area.

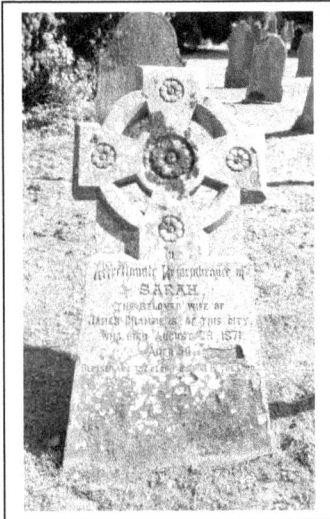
The grave of Sarah Chambers (nee Jones)
At Hereford Cemetery

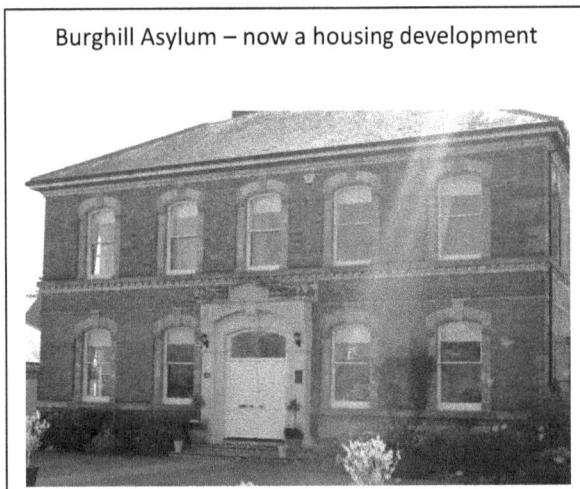
Burghill Asylum – now a housing development

Several original buildings and green spaces still exist alongside new homes of similar design

James must have been one of the earliest patients at the 'Hereford County and City Lunatic Asylum' at Burghill, just outside Hereford. It was built in 1868, replacing the old Hereford Asylum. It covered 10 acres, with a further 100 acres of gardens, a farm and several cottages. The main asylum was divided into two blocks to separate men and women, each wing able to take 200 patients. The male block had a workshop and brewhouse, the female block, a laundry. As well as spaces for dining and recreation, there was a chapel. Gas, for the lighting, was provided from a gasworks in the grounds.

A report from the 'Committee of Visitors', in the 1880s, seems to show that the asylum was a well-run establishment, stating that the absence of deaths linked to homicide or suicide demonstrated the level of careful supervision maintained over the patients.

There are signs that James started to engage with the gardener, occupying himself in the greenhouse, hopefully influenced by the tranquil setting and care he received. James Chambers died at the asylum in 1907, aged 79. He had been a patient for over forty years.

The 'Burghill Lunatic Asylum' eventually changed its name to 'St Mary's Hospital', named after the parish in which it was situated. Now, St Mary's Lane winds past a number of the original, Grade 2 listed buildings and the new houses that coexist. The modern buildings have been carefully designed to incorporate similar fancy brickwork and slate roofs. Unusually, the green spaces have been maintained and the plot sizes appear generous. The estate feels quiet and calm, an aspiration that might have been behind its much earlier blue print.

The Rowcliffes

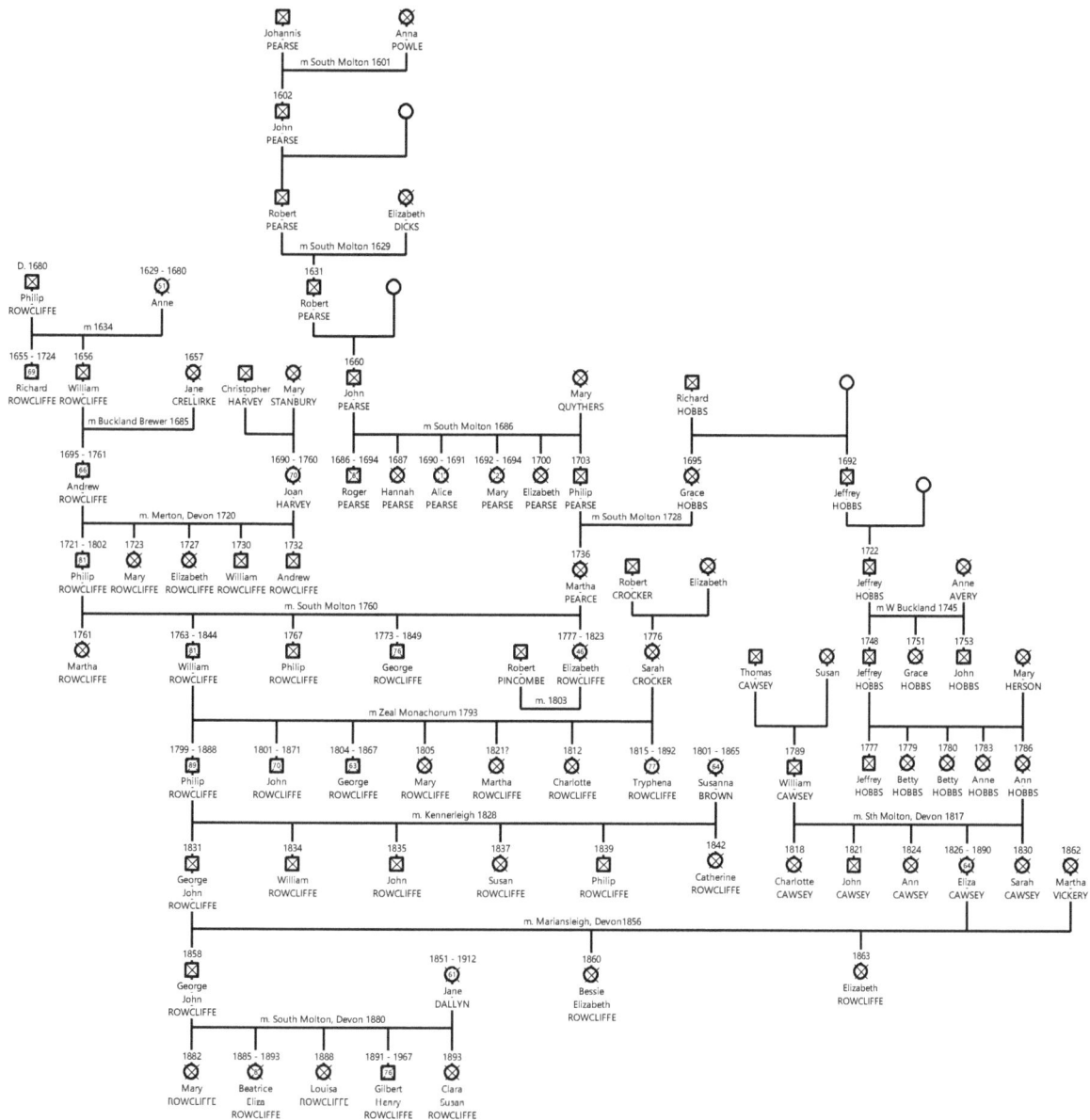

Family tree diagram

- Johannis PEARSE — Anna POWLE — m South Molton 1601
- 1602 John PEARSE
- Robert PEARSE — Elizabeth DICKS — m South Molton 1629
- 1631 Robert PEARSE

- D. 1680 Philip ROWCLIFFE — 1629 - 1680 Anne — m 1634
- 1660 John PEARSE — Mary QUYTHERS
- Richard HOBBS

- 1655 - 1724 Richard ROWCLIFFE
- 1656 William ROWCLIFFE
- 1657 Jane CRELLIRKE
- Christopher HARVEY — Mary STANBURY — m Buckland Brewer 1685
- m South Molton 1686

- 1695 - 1761 Andrew ROWCLIFFE
- 1690 - 1760 Joan HARVEY
- 1686 - 1694 Roger PEARSE
- 1687 Hannah PEARSE
- 1690 - 1691 Alice PEARSE
- 1692 - 1694 Mary PEARSE
- 1700 Elizabeth PEARSE
- 1703 Philip PEARSE
- 1695 Grace HOBBS
- 1692 Jeffrey HOBBS
- m. Merton, Devon 1720
- m South Molton 1728

- 1721 - 1802 Philip ROWCLIFFE
- 1723 Mary ROWCLIFFE
- 1727 Elizabeth ROWCLIFFE
- 1730 William ROWCLIFFE
- 1732 Andrew ROWCLIFFE
- 1736 Martha PEARCE
- Robert CROCKER
- Elizabeth
- 1722 Jeffrey HOBBS
- Anne AVERY
- m W Buckland 1745
- m. South Molton 1760

- 1761 Martha ROWCLIFFE
- 1763 - 1844 William ROWCLIFFE
- 1767 Philip ROWCLIFFE
- 1773 - 1849 George ROWCLIFFE
- Robert PINCOMBE
- 1777 - 1823 Elizabeth ROWCLIFFE
- 1776 Sarah CROCKER
- m. 1803
- Thomas CAWSEY
- Susan
- 1748 Jeffrey HOBBS
- 1751 Grace HOBBS
- 1753 John HOBBS
- Mary HERSON
- m Zeal Monachorum 1793

- 1799 - 1888 Philip ROWCLIFFE
- 1801 - 1871 John ROWCLIFFE
- 1804 - 1867 George ROWCLIFFE
- 1805 Mary ROWCLIFFE
- 1821? Martha ROWCLIFFE
- 1812 Charlotte ROWCLIFFE
- 1815 - 1892 Tryphena ROWCLIFFE
- 1801 - 1865 Susanna BROWN
- 1789 William CAWSEY
- 1777 Jeffrey HOBBS
- 1779 Betty HOBBS
- 1780 Betty HOBBS
- 1783 Anne HOBBS
- 1786 Ann HOBBS
- m. Kennerleigh 1828
- m. Sth Molton, Devon 1817

- 1831 George John ROWCLIFFE
- 1834 William ROWCLIFFE
- 1835 John ROWCLIFFE
- 1837 Susan ROWCLIFFE
- 1839 Philip ROWCLIFFE
- 1842 Catherine ROWCLIFFE
- 1818 Charlotte CAWSEY
- 1821 John CAWSEY
- 1824 Ann CAWSEY
- 1826 - 1890 Eliza CAWSEY
- 1830 Sarah CAWSEY
- 1862 Martha VICKERY
- m. Mariansleigh, Devon 1856

- 1858 George John ROWCLIFFE
- 1851 - 1912 Jane DALLYN
- 1860 Bessie Elizabeth ROWCLIFFE
- 1863 Elizabeth ROWCLIFFE
- m. South Molton, Devon 1880

- 1882 Mary ROWCLIFFE
- 1885 - 1893 Beatrice Eliza ROWCLIFFE
- 1888 Louisa ROWCLIFFE
- 1891 - 1967 Gilbert Henry ROWCLIFFE
- 1893 Clara Susan ROWCLIFFE

The Rowcliffe name was first found in Lancashire, at Radcliffe, a parish in Salford around the time of the Domesday Book of 1086, where it was listed as Radecliue.

The ancient Devonshire Rowcliffe family lived at Yarnscombe, eight miles from Merton. William Rockley of Yarnscombe married Jone Bagbeare of Bagbeare and they had four sons and one daughter: Thomas, born 1554, George, born 1555, John, Aldered and Emma (recorded in the Visitations of Devon 1620).

The recurring names in the family are George, Philip and William. Unfortunately, many of the Devon records were lost in a bombing during the World War II, however, the following is, I believe, accurate.

It is not clear yet how Philip Rowcliffe, Bill's 8xG Grandfather links to the Rowcliffe family of the 'visitations', that is a problem still to be solved. What is known, is that Philip and his wife Anne, had sons Richard and William. William then married Jane Crellirke of Buckland Brewer and their son Andrew was born in 1695.

Still within the area of Merton, North Devon, Andrew Rowcliffe, aged 25 years, married Joan Harvey. They had five children: Philip, Mary, Elizabeth, William and Andrew. The family were both landowners and farmers of significant holdings as 'occupiers' (the word used at the time for tenant farmers). Philip, Bill's 5xG Grandfather, being the eldest son, would have been the heir to the majority of his father's property.

Philip married in South Molton, the village home of his wife Martha Pearce, in 1760. Martha was the daughter of Philip Pearce, whose profession is recorded in the purchase of a property in South Molton as 'husbandman of property', possibly a landlord. The couple settled in King's Nympton and then moved to Bishop's Nympton in around 1770. They had five children: Martha, William (Bill's 4xG Grandfather), Philip, George and Elizabeth (Betty), who married Robert Pincombe (brother of my 4xG Grandfather, John). The sons all continued the family path and were Yeomen, farming in the areas of King's Nympton and Bishop's Nympton.

William married Sarah Crocker of Zeal Monachorum, the daughter of Robert and Elizabeth Crocker, in 1793. They had seven children: three sons followed by four daughters. Philip, John and George, all born in Chumleigh, Mary and Martha, born in Bishop's Nympton and then Charlotte and Tryphena, born in Witheridge.

Their son, Philip, married Susanna Brown, of Kennerleigh, in 1828. They made their home at Cobley Farm, Lapford, where Philip was a 'Yeoman' farmer. The couple had six children, born between 1831 and 1842: George (baptised George John Brown Rowcliffe), William, John, Susan, Philip and Catherine. Philip's father William, mother Sarah and the rest of the family lived at East Emlett, Woolfardisworthy. After William's death, in 1844, his wife, Sarah, and Philip's unmarried brothers and sisters (then in their 40s) remained there.

Philip, as eldest son, might have benefitted from his father William's will. The East Emlett estate was some 230 acres. As the eldest son of the eldest son, his inheritance could have been considerable. However, evidence does not seem to verify this.

His brothers John and George had both been named in the wills of their uncles, Philip and George.

Their Uncle George had no children of his own. In his Will, he left them:

'All those my messuages tenements mills and farms commonly called or known by the names of Bridge Mole Mills Little Heale Mole Park and West Silcombe situated lying and being in the several parishes of Rose Ash and Bishops Nympton ... also all other my freehold copyhold and leasehold messuages lands tenements and hereditaments and real estate situated in the parishes of Rose Ash and Bishops Nympton aforesaid and elsewhere And also All my Goods Chattels and Personal Estate and Property.'

Uncle Philip's son John was the heir to the majority of his estate, but he left his daughter Charlotte and his nephews John and George, £500 each.

Although his brothers inherited 'Little Heale', it was Philip who moved to that farm, with its fifty acres. The Tithe record however, shows that Philip was actually a tenant farmer, and the farm was owned by a third party, not either of his brothers. His sons all grew up working on the 'Little Heale' (or Little Hill) Farm, in Bishop's Nympton. Susanna died in 1865, but their son Philip and daughter Susan remained on the farm, unmarried, until Philip died, aged 89. He had out-lived a number of his children and when, at the age of 78, he was summoned by the Board of Guardians to pay five shillings a week for the maintenance of three of his grandchildren, who had become chargeable to the Union, he explained that he was already keeping one fatherless child, and that his farm was a very small one. He agreed, however to contribute one shilling.

Philip's son George John Brown Rowcliffe worked as a farm labourer at Garliford Farm, in Bishop's Nympton, the farm of William Elsworthy. He married Eliza Cossey (or Cawsey), of South Molton, where they set up home. Neither could write their own name, and the marriage certificate is 'signed' with their respective marks (a simple cross was required). George and Eliza had three children: George, after his father, Eliza, after her mother (called Betsy or Bessie) and Elizabeth. George (senior) continued to work as a farm labourer. Their son George took up an apprenticeship with Gilbert Babbage, a butcher in the neighbouring village of Alswear, later working as a butcher in South Molton. Their daughter Bessie, took work as a dressmaker, probably working from home, and Elizabeth worked as a general day servant.

It was in South Molton that George (junior) met Jane, daughter of another farm labourer, George Dallyn. They married in 1880, and initially, remained living in George's family home, with his father George, mother Eliza and two sisters. The couple had a daughter, Mary, in 1882 and it can be imagined that this made the small house feel rather cramped.

In 1883, at the age of 24 years, George took the decision to enlist with the Army Service Corps. It cannot be known whether this decision was driven by financial pressure, the discomfort of living in restricted conditions or a feeling of national duty. At that time, young men were not generally accepted into the ASC, if married. It then is of little surprise that in his 'Short Service Attestation' papers he reported that he was unmarried. George enlisted at Aldershot in his profession as butcher. His contract was to work as 'butcher soldier' for 12 years. This was made up of three-and-a-half years at the army base with the remaining time as an army reserve.

George and Jane had a further daughter, Beatrice, in 1885. Two years later, at the end of George's period at the army base, the couple moved to their own small accommodation in Stedifords Court, East Street. It was there that their third daughter, Louisa, was born. George took on premises in Barnstaple Street, in South Molton, for his butcher's shop.

Eliza died, aged 64, between July and September 1890, and this seemed to mark a turn of events for George Rowcliffe (senior). He remarried, a 29-year-old local woman, Martha, before the end of that year. Martha was the daughter of William Vickers (himself five years younger than George), farmer of 150 acres, in nearby West Buckland. By the time of the 1891 Census, George and Martha were living at Bradford Farm, Braunton, were he is recorded as 'farmer', working for himself (on own account). This he did, until his death in 1909. It seems a shame for Martha, that she had had no children of her own. She was 46 years old when she became a widow. However, financially, she seemed secure. She moved to a house in West Down, near Braunton, where she had a live-in 'general servant'.

George Rowcliffe (junior) continued as a butcher, in South Molton, the family home remained in East Street. Jane contributed to the family income with her dressmaking. The couple had five children in all: Mary, Beatrice, who died aged just eight years, Louisa (Lucy), Gilbert and Clara. Family stories tell of how George was not ideally suited to his profession. He hated killing the livestock and consumed a fair amount of alcohol before attempting the task. He would then slaughter the animals in the evening while poor Lucy was made to hold the lamp.

It was in 1900, that the family were to see a major change. George left them. According to family members, 'he simply disappeared'.

By 1901, Jane had taken over as butcher and lived with twelve-year-old Louisa, ten-year-old Gilbert and eight-year-old Clara. Daughter Mary had moved to Coventry and was working as an elementary school teacher.

Mary nee Rowcliffe and William Hopkins

Mary, remained in Coventry and married William Hopkins. She gave up teaching to look after their growing family of four daughters and one son: Marjorie, Daisy, Alice, Marie and George. Marie followed her mother into teaching, whilst George became a pharmacist.

Gilbert Rowcliffe with nieces Daisy and Marjorie Hopkins

Gilbert joined the Royal Engineers at the age of 18. In 1919, following World War 1, he married Edith Davis, a nurse from Tenbury, Wells. They began married life in Tenbury and some years later, settled in Wolverhampton with their three sons: Harry, David and Geoffrey.

David Rowcliffe with Edie, his mother

Sadly, Geoffrey died in a tragic accident, when his bike was stuck by a trolley bus, at the age of 14. Then in 1944, the family suffered the loss of David. At just 21 years of age, he was killed in action, a fight sergeant navigator with 49 Squadron, RAF. Harry married Doreen Evans in 1955 and they continued to live in Wolverhampton into their old age.

Clara went to work as housemaid for the Rector at Warkleigh Rectory, in Umberleigh, just a few miles away from South Molton. She married Ivor Dallimore, a coal hewer, in 1920 and settled in Monmouthshire, Wales. Clara and Ivor had two children: Thelma and Ernest, both born in Aberbargoed.

Clara died in Bradford, Yorkshire, aged 75 years.

Clara Rowcliffe

By 1911, Jane and the only daughter remaining at home, Louisa, had moved to Waterloo Place, a few doors away from their previous home, in East Street. Jane by this time was an 'invalid', cared for by her 22-year-old daughter.

Jane Rowcliffe (nee Dallyn) and daughter (possibly Louisa)

Louisa continued to care for her mother until her mother's death, in 1912.

Jane Rowcliffe (nee Dallyn)

It is now possible to see that during the same time period, George had travelled to Bristol, where he had signed up for a second short period with the Army Service Corps. This time it was for one year, again based in this country. In the absence of a photograph, George's medical notes give a little insight into his appearance. He was of relatively short stature, being 5ft 6in tall, with a weight of 160 lbs. He had blue/grey eyes and brown hair. A scar on his left thumb and the loss of his molar teeth were his only 'distinguishing marks'. He worked as a butcher at the army base in Aldershot

In 1901, at the end of his service, instead of returning to his wife in Devon, George moved to Glamorganshire, in South Wales. It appears that he settled in Swansea, for that is where he met single woman Sarah Jane Russ, 22 years his junior. Sarah Jane was the eldest daughter of watchman Frederick Russ and his wife Eliza. Sarah had been working for the Rogers family as a general domestic servant.

In 1906, Sarah gave birth to a daughter, Eliza. Her birth was registered Eliza Lilian Russ. George and Sarah Jane stayed together and moved to Aberaman, in the Rhondda Valley. Their home was at 174, Cardiff Road. A strange coincidence, is that Cardiff Road (albeit a different number) would also be home to George's grand-daughter Glenys. Here, George and Sarah had their second child, a son, Frederick. His birth was registered Frederick George John Rowcliffe, even though the couple were unmarried (George still being married to Jane). At the time of Frederick's baptism, George was working as a butcher in the area. When daughter Ida Elizabeth was born, in 1910, they had moved to Blaencwn, a village just outside Aberdare, where George was still finding work as a butcher. When the 1911 Census return was completed, they had moved again to the village of Trealaw, a few miles away. The report shows that George had reduced the difference in the couple's ages by knocking a total of eight years from his 49. Also, although all but Eliza had had their births registered with the surname Rowcliffe, the document has them all as Russ. Although still a single woman, Sarah declared herself 'widow' and 'housekeeper' for the Census record. George himself, had found work as a 'repairer underground' in a coalmine in the Rhondda Valley.

Subsequently, in 1912, Daisy was born and her birth was again registered as Rowcliffe, despite the fact that the couple were still unmarried (they would have been unaware of Jane's very recent death). Interestingly, all the children assumed their father's surname in later years.

Following her mother Jane's death, it is not yet clear why Louisa then made her way to Hereford, where she met widower Richard Kinnersley. Richard's wife had died in 1914, leaving him with three young children to care for, the youngest, just eight years old. Perhaps that was the role she had embarked upon.

The couple obviously became close and, in the early summer of 1918, Louisa found herself pregnant and unmarried, at that time, still a circumstance that was severely frowned upon. They promptly married, but tragically, before their baby had been born, Richard died in the unremitting influenza epidemic that was sweeping the country. Louisa must have felt so alone with her grief and no doubt desperately worried about how she might look after her baby. She gave birth to Edith Mary, Bill's mother, in October 1918. Richard's other children, Edgar Doris and Gwendoline had had little time to accept Louisa as their step-mother. They were taken in by one of Richard's sisters.

Louisa moved to Wales. At first, it seemed that she may have had some idea about the whereabouts of her father George Rowcliffe and his second family, because her home became Glamorganshire, in South Wales. However, those who knew her, believe this was not the case. Apparently, the family always maintained that George had 'just disappeared'.

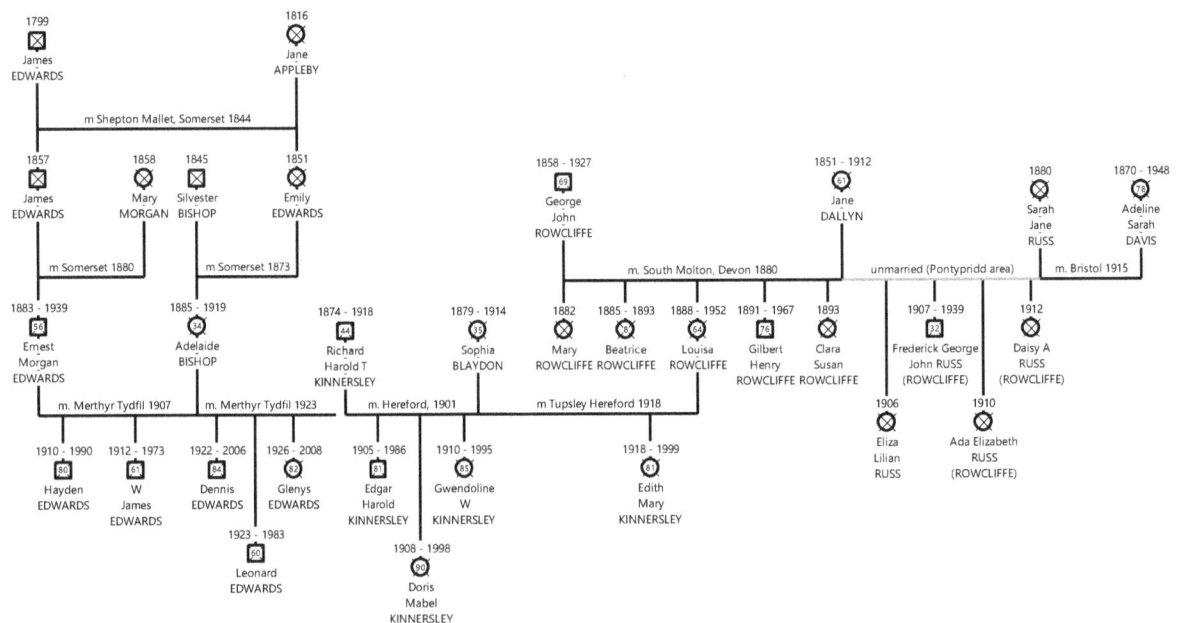

Ernest Edwards had been born in Evercreech, Somerset. He and his brother Walter took up work as miners, in Aberdare, during a major recruitment drive, between 1906 and 1908. The brothers settled in Aberaman, living next door to each other, with their respective wives, in Mason Street. Ernest had married Adelaide Bishop, his first cousin.

Sadly, like Louisa, Ernest also lost his spouse, 34-year-old Adelaide, at the very beginning of 1919. He had two young boys to care for, aged seven and nine. It is now known that Louisa answered Ernest's advertisement for a housekeeper. She was offered and accepted the post. Louisa and Ernest, both widowed, married just six weeks later, in 1921. Together they had three more children, Dennis, Leonard and finally Glenys.

Edie Kinnersley (about 3 years) with step brothers Jim and Haydn Edwards.

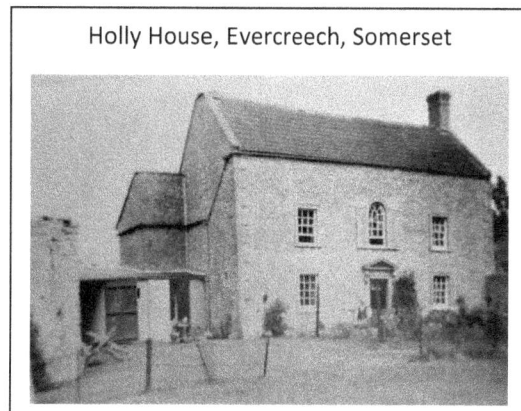

Holly House, Evercreech, Somerset

It must have been lovely for the children to live so close to their Uncle Walter, Aunt Rosina (Rose) and cousins Hubert (known as Ken, his middle name) and Gordon. This is the way things were until 1936, when Walter and Ernest's mother died. Walter and his family decided to return to Somerset, to live with James Edwards, their father. Their home, Holly House, in Evercreech, then became a favourite place for extended visits.

From the records, it appears that George Rowcliffe, when free to marry, actually left his second young family. Instead, he went to Bristol where in 1914 he enlisted again with the Army Service Corps, to serve in World War 1 as a 'butcher soldier'. Although, as with many records, his enlistment papers were lost in the bombings of World War 2, a medal awarded on discharge attests to the fact that George had again falsified his age. On enlisting, he had taken twelve years from his 56, making himself 44 years old. It is likely that he would have been refused entry had he given his correct age.

Surprisingly, in 1915, he married Adeline Davis. Adeline, born in Banwell, Somerset, was working in Bristol for the Hemmons family, as a domestic servant. The marriage took place in Bristol and their marriage certificate shows George's address at the time as 'Hazeldene' South Street, Lancing, Sussex.

It can be assumed that he was working at the army base in Lancing. Again, his age was wrongly recorded as 47, just two years older than Adeline. In fact, he was 57!

Soon after their marriage, it appears that George was posted overseas. Then, in March 1916, he was discharged due to poor health. Corporal George Rowcliffe was awarded the 'Silver War Badge', the record of which still survives. The reason for discharge is given as:

'Sickness Para of King's Regulation 392 (xvi)'

This means he was unfit to continue in his role.

When the 1921 Census is released for viewing, it may be possible to see whether George returned to Adeline. For now, all that can be reliably recorded is that he made Hereford his home and that is where he died in 1927. However, there is a further twist in the story of George John Rowcliffe. His death certificate states that he died of 'Broncho Pneumonia' leading to 'Cardiac Failure' while at the Hereford Hospital. Prior to admission, he had been living at 3, St Nicholas Street, a boarding house, in Hereford, quite close to the Cathedral, still working as a butcher.

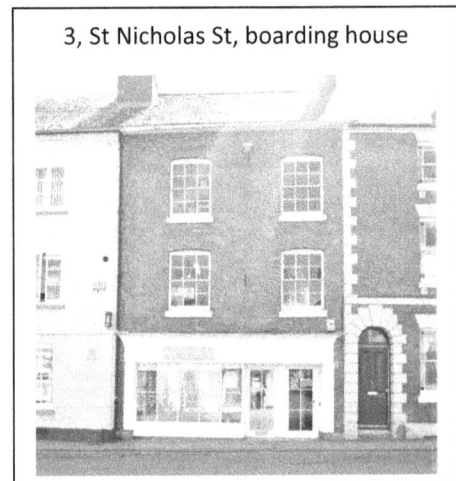

3, St Nicholas St, boarding house

Present at his death and the informant of the death, was Gilbert, his son by first wife Jane. Gilbert then, must have been in contact with his father. This leaves a huge question mark over whether others in the family were in contact with George. Did Gilbert's sisters really think that George had 'just disappeared' or were they trying to distance themselves from his rather sorry story?

The final twist is that George's total estate of £31 15s 4d was inherited by his 'wife' Fannie. There is no record of this 'marriage'. His grave is at the Hereford Cemetery.

Just to pick up on some of those affected along the way;

Sarah (George's second partner) continued to be known as Sarah Rowcliffe. She finally married a Henry Davies, in 1919.

Adeline Rowcliffe did not remarry. She died in 1948.

Eliza, Ida and Daisy, George's daughters with Sarah Jane, all married. Sadly, their son Frederick was killed in a shipping accident in 1939, on board the merchant ship 'Prestatyn Rose'.

Louisa and Ernest's children Dennis, Leonard and Glenys were all born and grew up in Glamorganshire.

Left to Right:

Glenis (nee Edwards) and Desmond Kerley,
Edie Rowcliffe (nee Davis),
Louisa Edwards (nee Rowcliffe),
Leonard Edwards
(A neighbour, Mrs Coles, is behind Leonard)

Dennis Edwards (left) and Leonard Edwards (right)

Louisa Edwards (nee Rowcliffe) -seated

Despite being step sister and half-sister to her siblings, it was obvious that Edie thought the world of them all.

Edith Mary Kinnersley (Edie)

On leaving school, Edie secured a haberdashery apprenticeship with 'Powell and Sons', a draper's shop in Aberaman. I remember her saying how much she had enjoyed the work, particularly the window dressing. She stayed in the same employment for four years. We still have a glowing reference for her, written by the proprietor some years later.

War was declared on 5th September 1939 and as a direct result of this, a register was taken that listed the personal details of every civilian in Great Britain. It was an important tool in coordinating the war effort at home. The enumerators issued identity cards as they collected the information, which was also used to organise rationing. At the time of the register, 29th September, Edie was living at 'Vale View' in Wincanton, Somerset, where she had found work as a household assistant to retired couple, Ernest and Ida Knapman.

Dennis had been living at Holly House and family recollections are that Edie joined him there for a time.

Sadly, Ernest Edwards, Edie's dearly loved step father, died before the end of 1939. Louisa was left a widow for the second time. She worked hard to try to 'make ends meet' and the family benefitted from being part of a close-knit and supportive community. Nevertheless, it was a time when there was huge financial pressure.

Edie married Bill Rees, an RAF engineer, in February 1940. After a short time together, Bill had to return to duty and Edie remained in Aberdare. It was there that their first son was born.

In 1945, Bill left the RAF and returned to Aberdare where he took engineering work at the 'Cable Works'. This was around the time of the birth of their second son. Subsequently, Bill started to work for the Air Ministry, over time, working in a number of locations. One move was to Pershore, in Worcestershire, where their third son was born.

There were to be many more moves ahead, most were embarked upon with enthusiasm and Edie rose to the challenge of making each house a suitable home for the boys. She always looked back fondly at the time they spent in Pershore, saying that the house was 'ahead of its time' with its modern layout and facilities. The move from there was perhaps the hardest for her.

In 1952, Louisa died aged 63 years. The facts tell of a life that had not been easy, but from the glimpses we have of her, it is clear that she was a determined and resourceful woman. The newspaper obituary describes her as 'of a quiet and unassuming disposition'. She had only been ill for three days, so her passing was a shock for the family.

Ernest had been buried with Adelaide, his first wife, at the Aberdare Cemetery. Louisa was laid to rest with them.

The Dallyns

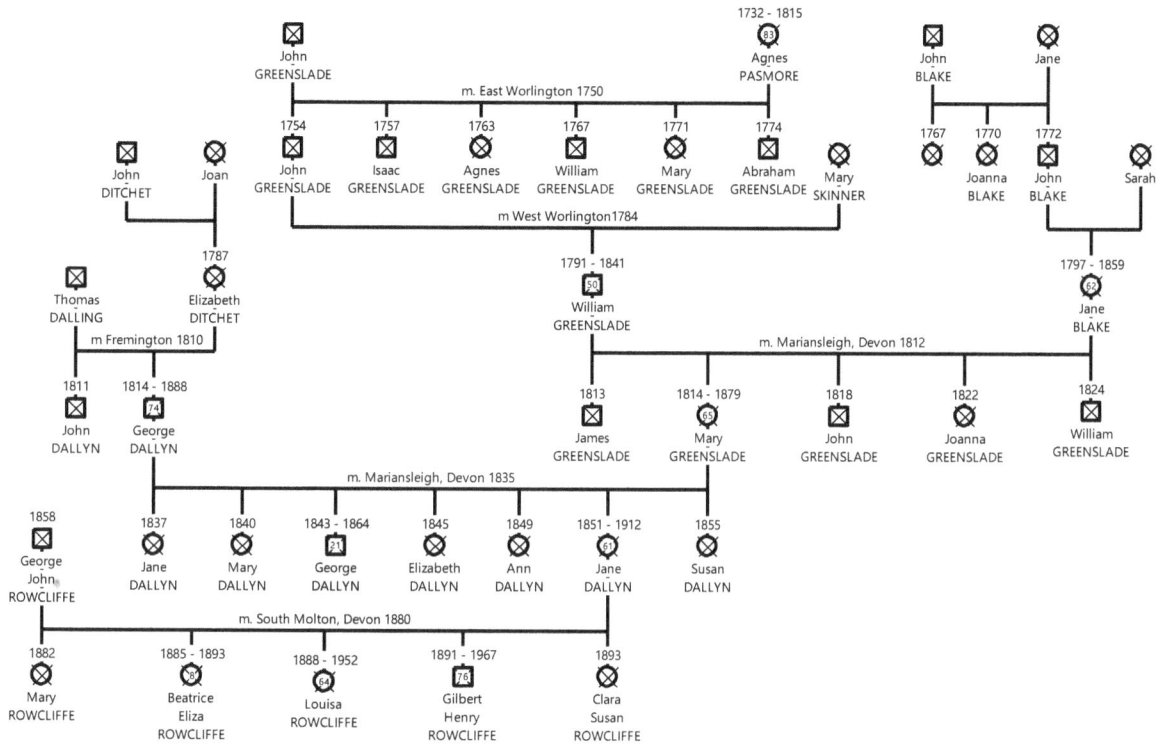

The Dallyn family had a long history of farming in North Devon and descendants are still farming in the area today. The acreage covered was vast, some were working farms as tenant farmers and some as land-owners.

George Dallyn

George Dallyn was not one of the brothers owning land but worked as a farm labourer all his life. He married Mary, in 1835, the daughter of William Greenslade. Following William's death in 1841, George and Mary moved to East Street, in South Molton. It is likely that they took over the occupancy of William's former house. George's brother John, another farm labourer, and his family were also living in East Street. Sadly, the couple's first baby, Jane after her mother, died soon after birth. Their family however, was to grow, and the couple went on to have another five daughters and just the one son: Mary, George, Elizabeth, Ann, Jane and Susan.

Their only son, George, took work as a 'labouring tanner' at Wheatland farm, in North Molton. It must have caused them great sadness when he died aged just 21. Their daughters worked as weavers until their respective marriages. It was Jane who stayed longest with her parents. Her mother, Mary died in 1879 and Jane married George Rowcliffe the following year. Her father, George Dallyn, then working as a tanner, moved to a larger house that became available across the road in East Street. His youngest daughter Susan, her husband and young family moved in with him. Susan had married John Bowden a 'painter (workman)' and was herself taking in work as a dressmaker.

George Dallyn died in 1888, aged 74. He was buried in the South Molton Cemetery, with his wife Mary and daughter Ann. Two further children, Jane and George, were also buried there, but unfortunately, the headstones are no longer in situ. Bill and I were helped to find the location of the graves, now lawned areas with the original dividing paths.

The Gravestone at South Molton Cemetery, for George, Mary and daughter Ann Dallyn

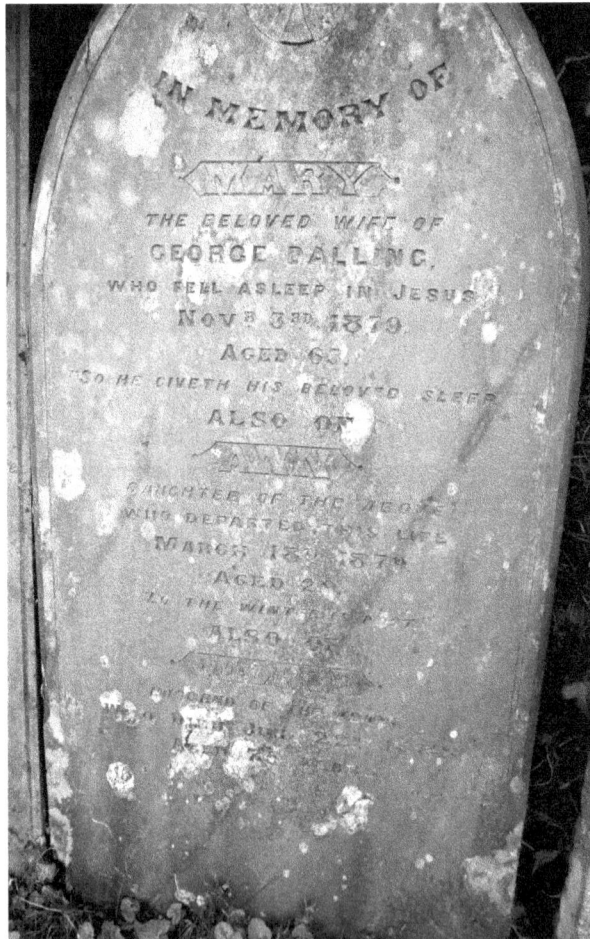

The Rees and Jones Families

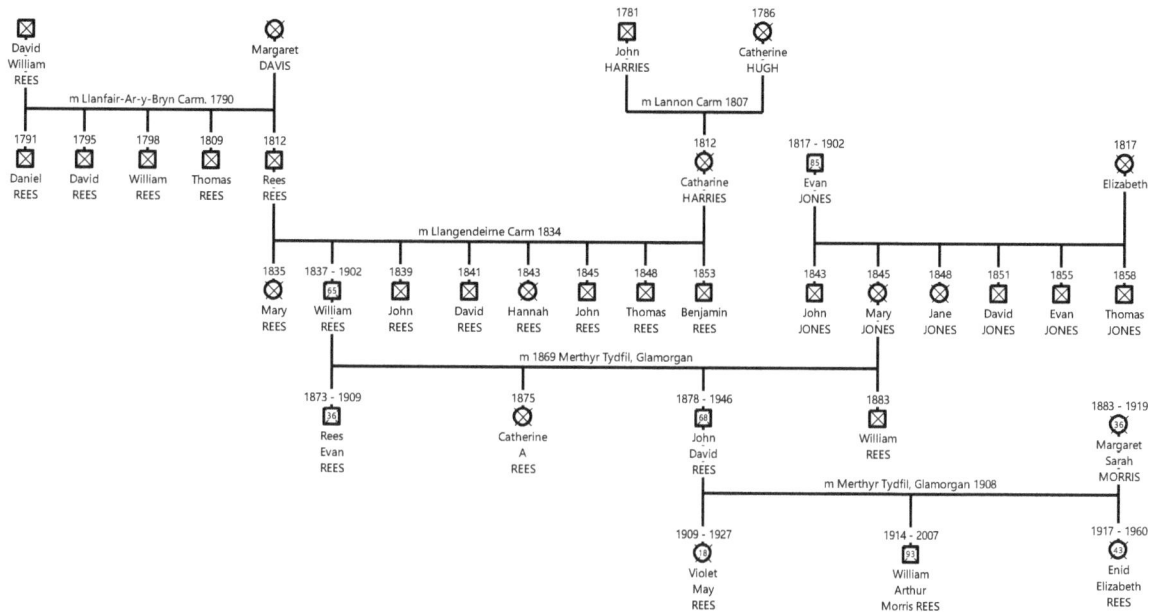

Genealogical chart of the Rees and Jones Families

David William REES — **Margaret DAVIS**
m Llanfair-Ar-y-Bryn Carm. 1790

1781 John HARRIES — **1786 Catherine HUGH**
m Lannon Carm 1807

- 1791 Daniel REES
- 1795 David REES
- 1798 William REES
- 1809 Thomas REES
- 1812 Rees REES
- 1812 Catharine HARRIES
- 1817–1902 Evan JONES
- 1817 Elizabeth

m Llangendeirne Carm 1834

- 1835 Mary REES
- 1837–1902 William REES
- 1839 John REES
- 1841 David REES
- 1843 Hannah REES
- 1845 John REES
- 1848 Thomas REES
- 1853 Benjamin REES
- 1843 John JONES
- 1845 Mary JONES
- 1848 Jane JONES
- 1851 David JONES
- 1855 Evan JONES
- 1858 Thomas JONES

m 1869 Merthyr Tydfil, Glamorgan

- 1873–1909 Rees Evan REES
- 1875 Catherine A REES
- 1878–1946 John David REES
- 1883 William REES
- 1883–1919 Margaret Sarah MORRIS

m Merthyr Tydfil, Glamorgan 1908

- 1909–1927 Violet May REES
- 1914–2007 William Arthur Morris REES
- 1917–1960 Enid Elizabeth REES

Our Welsh ancestors have been particularly tricky to locate. Surnames were only introduced in Wales about 500 years ago. Before this, some names were derived from nicknames and a few from occupations. In the main, they managed by having a baptismal or first name and affixed to that by the particle 'ap' meaning 'son of', or 'ferch' meaning 'daughter of', they fixed their father's, grandfather's, great grandfather's names, going back up to eight or nine generations. So, for general purposes, a man might give his name as John, but to distinguish himself from others he would give his whole name, which included the first names of his ancestors, most recent first, for example 'John ap Rhys ap Llewelyn ap Gruffydd ap Dafydd ap Griffith ap Meilyr'.

This gave every person in Wales a genealogy, not just a name. According to the laws of Hywel Dda (Hywel the Good), land could not be held by individuals. They needed to prove that they were descendant of a forefather, many generations back, who held tribal lands.

When around 500 years ago, the Welsh were asked to adopt a system of surnames, they tended to continue the tradition of affixing the names of their fathers. So, Rees son of John, would be Rees Jones, John son of Gruffydd, would be John Griffiths. At the same time, there was a simplification of first names. People had become nervous about using the previous wide variety of pagan or Catholic devotional names, and a small number of safe names were used instead. There were a few safe Biblical names like John, David and Thomas and a few safe royal names like Edward, Richard and William.

At a time when there were few first names, the Welsh were adopting these names as surnames. It is as a direct result of this that there are so many Jones, Davis, Evans surnames. Our own Edwards, Rees, Jones, Morris and Harries were all derived in the same way. Welsh communities are full of families with the same surname, but who are completely unrelated.

So there lies my excuse for the lack of discovering more of our Welsh ancestors. Their place in our family is just as valid to the vast tapestry that is our history, but just not clearly identifiable at the current time.

From the Census returns it is possible to see the prevalence of Welsh, spoken by our ancestors. The Census form choice was; Welsh-speaking, English-speaking or both. As a general rule, if they were born before 1900, all of our Welsh ancestors spoke both Welsh and English. Those born in the twentieth century tended to speak only English.

Our Welsh forebears are perhaps those that most demonstrate the effects of the 'Industrial Revolution'. In the mid 1700s, Wales was overwhelmingly rural. Most of Bill's identifiable 3xG Grandfathers were involved in farming. The 'Industrial Revolution' saw the country gradually expand its industrial base. By the early 1800s, industries that had been established during the reign of Elizabeth I expanded considerably. Coalmining in west Glamorgan and Flintshire, Silver and lead mining in Cardiganshire and Flintshire, Iron-making in Bersham and Pontypool and copper smelting in Swansea and Neath all increased substantially.

This increase was still marginal when compared with the agricultural economy. Agriculture had itself developed with the use of lime and the adoption of crop rotation. Factory methods were also replacing domestic production in the woollen industry. However, by 1851, two thirds of the population were supported by work other than in agriculture, and Wales was the world's second most industrial nation, after England.

North-east Wales developed the widest range of industries. By 1800 there were 19 metalworks, 14 potteries, cotton mills, lead and coal mines and one of Europe's leading ironworks.

It was in the south though, over time, that developments were the most important. Llanelli, Swansea and Neath saw significant economic development. The Cyfarthfa and Dowlais ironworks in Merthyr Tydfil made this Wales's first industrial town. By the 1830s Monmouthshire and Glamorgan were producing half of the iron exported by Britain. By the 1850s none of Bill's ancestors were involved in farming.

Rees Rees, Bill's 2xG Grandfather was born in 1812, in LLangendeirne, near Swansea, Carmarthenshire. His father was a farmer in the Carmarthenshire countryside. Rather than agricultural work, Rees himself took work as a copper man at the LLangyfelach Copperworks. This was the largest copperworks in Swansea. Workers could expect to take on a variety of different tasks relating to the heating of the metal, rolling the copper into sheets and hammering the sheets into shape.

Rees met Catharine, a young woman from Llangathen, Carmarthenshire. Her father, John Harries, was another farmer. The couple married in 1834, and settled in Llangyfelach, Swansea. Their children were born at Catharine's parents' home, 'Pwll yr air', not far from their own home. The eight children were: Mary, William, John (who died in childhood), David, Hannah, John, Thomas and Benjamin. It was Catharine's mother, another Catharine, who registered the births.

The children grew up in Swansea. Rees and Catharine's eldest daughter Mary, married John Jenkins and had two little daughters, Lydia and Catherine. Sadly, Mary died while the girls were very young. Her husband, John, moved into the Rees family home, no doubt this helped him with childcare so that he could continue to work. Rees and Catherine moved house towards the end of the 1850s. This may have been driven by the need for more space for their extended family, but it is probably more likely that, having completed their schooling, there was more work for the boys in Aberdare. The large coal mines at Aberdare and the world-renowned iron works at Merthyr Tydfil would present ample opportunities for employment. All eleven of them made Upper Colliers Row, Aberdare, their home. Upper and Lower Colliers Row were terraces of houses, almost exclusively occupied by miners.

Rees left the copperworks to work in the coalmines of Aberdare. William followed him into the mines. David and John Jenkins took up work at the iron works as puddlers, one of the most dangerous jobs available. Puddling was the process of converting pig iron into wrought iron with the use of a furnace. The men worked as a crew of two, a puddler and helper. Between them they could produce around 3300 pounds (1,500 kg) of iron in the twelve-hour shift. The overpowering heat and fumes coupled with the strenuous labour, as well as the frequency of accidents, caused puddlers to have a very short life expectancy, with most dying in their thirties. John died in his early forties. David became a coalminer.

By 1881, Rees and Catharine's sons were married, all still engaged in work at the mine. Three of the sons were living in Colliers Row: William and Mary's family at number 10, Thomas and Anne's family at number 16 and Benjamin and Mary's family at number 18. Their children were attending the local school at Abernant. John and Mary's family were a short distance away, at Bwllfa Row.

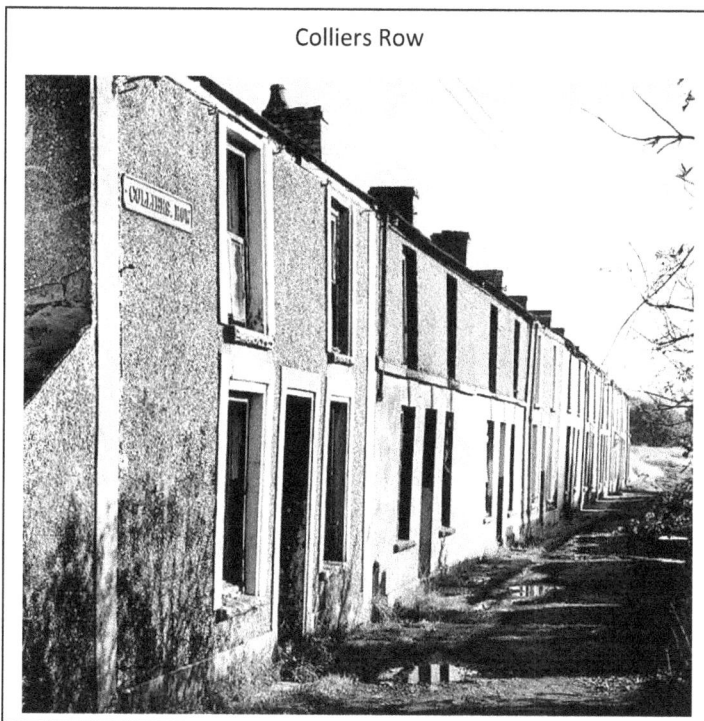
Colliers Row

William, Bill's Great Grandfather, had married Mary Jones in 1869. Mary was from Newquay, in Cardiganshire, West Wales. They married in Aberdare, Mary 'signing' her name with a cross. They named their first-born son Rees, after William's father, but added Evan as a middle name. Rees was followed by Catharine, after William's mother, and John, after Mary's father. William (junior) was their youngest child.

The Abernant school admission records show William's son Rees Evan Rees, and Benjamin's son Rees Rees, both starting school on January 27th 1879, at almost seven years of age. The boys were just two months apart in age. It must have been a little confusing for the poor infant teacher having two Rees Rees's in the same class, although in Wales it may not have been as unusual as it might seem.

William had followed his father into the mines and worked as a master haulier. His job as a 'haulier' would have meant being tasked with looking after the pit ponies. The ponies spent most of their life underground dragging wagons that were filled with coal, through narrow mine tunnels, so that it could be brought to the surface.

The South Wales coal mines adopted a system of issuing tokens to miners. Each miner was given a token with an identifying number on. When they collected their 'Davey lamp', every time they went down the mine, they would hand in the token. This meant that surface workers could keep a log of how many men were down the mine, and who they were, at any time. It was a dangerous occupation, major hazards being tunnel collapses and gas build-ups. The token system meant that, in the event of a problem occurring, there was a record of who was in the area.

William continued to work in the mines until his death, in 1902. However, he had made the change from working below ground and in 1901, was working as a lamp-man on the surface of the pit. William had not had much opportunity for education himself but was keen for his sons to benefit from the growing developments in training that were available in Cardiff.

Evening classes had been offered from 1841 by the Mechanics' Institute in Cardiff, but they were intermittent. The classes took place at Cardiff Free Library and came to be known as the School of Science. In the 1880s, the Government increased the provision of formal education beyond school. This was focussed on vocational 'technical' education. The Technical Instruction Act was passed in 1889, and the University College of South Wales and Monmouthshire (UCSWM) started to provide technical education. Two of the main aims of UCSWM (which was established in 1883) were, to ensure that education was offered to a wider audience than just full-time students, and to improve the education of the population of Wales generally, so this development was one they were keen to embrace. The institution became known as the Technical School of the County Borough of Cardiff.

William's sons all entered the mines. Rees Evan worked as an engine driver, John became a stationary engine driver and William, an engine fitter. Tragically, William died in his early twenties of tuberculosis. Rees Evan and John with the encouragement of their father, attended evening classes in electrical engineering. This gave them the skills needed to gain more technical employment.

Rees Evan moved to London, taking up work with the City of London Electric Lighting Company Limited. The company had been formed in July 1891, to generate and supply electricity to the City of London and part of north Southwark. It operated Bankside power station on the south bank of the river Thames.

John took on an important development role within the coal mines. This involved connecting electrical power to the mines, to drive the machinery and provide underground lighting.

Two main engineering problems had existed in underground mines. Firstly, the need to remove the underground water, to prevent flooding, and secondly, to develop sufficient ventilation below ground. Fresh air needed to be provided for the miners and also to prevent the build-up of methane gas, which had the potential to cause fires and explosions. Before the introduction of electricity, steam power was used to pump or lift the water out and to provide a simple ventilation system.

The introduction of electricity to the mines addressed these two main issues. It was also key to facilitating the use of electric coal-cutting machines and more efficient methods for transporting the coal to the surface.

Rees Evan Rees married Mary Owens, a young woman from Llancyfelin, Cardiganshire. Mary was the daughter of John Owens and Mary Jones. She had always lived on her grandfather's 90-acre farm, with her mother and eight aunts and uncles. The couple married in Bethnal Green, London, and their first daughter, Elizabeth, was born there. They had three further daughters, Jane, Gertrude and Catherine, all born in Walthamstow, West Ham, London, where they lived near the River Lea. Life in London, however, was to come to a sudden end when Rees Evan drowned in the River Lea, near Ponder's End Lock, aged 36. It seems that this was probably a tragic accident. Mary and the girls were unable to sustain themselves in London and so returned to Wales. Mary and her eldest daughter Elizabeth, were taken in by her brother James Jones, a cleric, living at the Llandinam Vicarage, Montgomeryshire. Her other daughters were given a home by their grandmother Mary Owens, by that time the owner of the farm where Mary had grown up. Two of Mary's aunts still lived at the farm and no doubt helped to look after the young girls.

Rees Evan and John's sister Catherine, married William Jenkins. They had a son in 1917, William John Jenkins. Born towards the end of the First World War, William Jenkins was destined to play a significant part in the Second World War. William was a private in the 4th Service Battalion, Welsh Regiment and was awarded the Military Medal for 'Bravery in the Field', in France.

John married Margaret Morris, known as Maggie, the daughter of Arthur Morris, in 1908. A report in the Aberdare Leader describes their wedding in some detail:

A very pretty and interesting wedding was solemnized on Sunday morning last at Carmel English Baptist Chapel, Aberdare, the happy pair being Mr. John D. Rees, electrician at The Marquis of Bute Collieries, Aberdare, and Miss Margaret (Maggie) Morris, eldest daughter of Mr. and Mrs. Arthur Morris, 17, Duke-street. The marriage was celebrated by the Rev. A. B. Kinsey, B.A., in the presence of Mr. Geo. G. Jones, Registrar, and the wedding was attended by a goodly number of Mr. and Mrs. Rees' friends. The bride, who was given away by her father, was charmingly attired in a travelling costume of navy-blue cloth and blue glace silk hat (trimmed with roses) to match. Mr. William Jenkins (Abernant), brother-in-law of the bridegroom, acted as best man; and the bride was attended by her bridesmaids, Miss Maude Morris, of Oxford (sister): Miss Flossie Morris, Llanelly, sister; Miss Dolly Morris, sister; Miss Emily Singleton (cousin), Miss Gertrude Davies, R.A.M., Llanelly (cousin), and Miss Minnie Edwards, also of Llanelly (cousin). Amongst others present were: Mrs. Agnes Smith, Llanelly (aunt of the bride), Messrs. David James Morris and Trevor Morris (brothers), Mrs. Jenkins (sister of the bridegroom), Miss Jennie Rees, of the Railway Bar Hotel; Miss D. Bryce, Compton House; Mr. Gwilym Mandry, Ystradgynlais; Mr. Fred Davies, Aberaman, and Mr. James Crowley, Aberdare. The whole of the party were afterwards entertained to a sumptuous breakfast at the home of the bride's parents, where all joined in best wishes for the happiness and prosperity of the happy pair. The wedding presents received by both bride and bridegroom were numerous and costly. The honeymoon is being spent at the Mumbles and elsewhere in West Wales. We extend to Mr. and Mrs. Rees our sincere congratulations.

Margaret Rees (nee Morris)

The couple moved in with Arthur Morris, his wife Elizabeth and their four other children. Space must have been tight, especially after the birth of Violet Mary (known as May). They lived at 17 Duke Street, both a shop and a home.

After moving to Gladstone Street, John and Maggie completed their family with the births of William Arthur Morris (known as Bill, his name a tribute to both grandfathers) and Enid Elizabeth.

John and Maggie made a further move to Windsor Villas, in Abernant. This was a larger house with good access to the Abernant School and colliery.

2, Windsor Villas, Abernant

In the latter part of 1918 and through into early 1919, the influenza epidemic that swept Britain claimed many lives. Sadly, one of those to succumb to the virus was Maggie. She died aged 35, leaving John with ten-year-old May, five-year-old William and two-year-old Enid. John managed initially with family help, especially from Maggie's sisters and Gertrude, daughter of his late brother Rees Evan. In the absence of their mother, the children became very close to Gertrude.

Gertrude Rees with William, in about 1915.

Gertrude was a caring young woman who became a significant part of the children's lives. She returned to London to study nursing at the Lambeth Hospital. Sadly, she died following an appendectomy in 1925, aged just 21 years.

May at Abernant School, aged 11

May is in the centre (with head leaning to one side)

Violet (May) with William (Bill) Rees

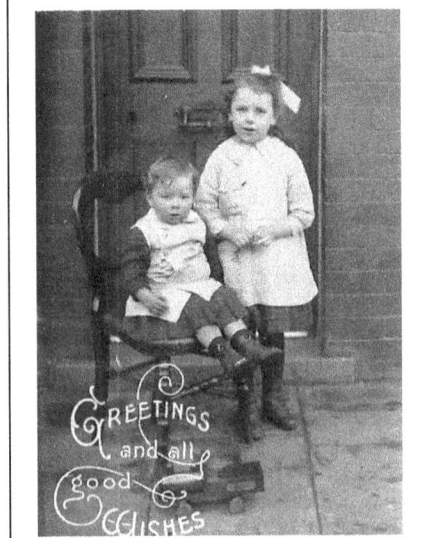

May's health deteriorated and when her doctor diagnosed tuberculosis, she was admitted to the Pontsarn Sanitorium. The hospital had been opened in 1913, specifically for the treatment of tuberculosis. The site had been chosen due to its sunny position and the protection it gave from cold north and east winds. Its 50 beds were moved outside in the summer to give the patients fresh air. May remain at the sanatorium for some months and Bill recounted his frequent long walks to visit his sister. Sadly, she died in 1927, aged just 18 years.

As a teenager, Bill and his sister Enid spent time with relatives of his paternal grandmother Mary (nee Jones), in New Quay, Cardiganshire. These seemed to be particularly happy times for Bill, as he recounted memories of the area in his later years. He remembered summer holidays staying in the 'White House' over-looking the bay and learning to carve wood under the tutelage of a relative who lived just outside New Quay, in a woodland cottage. Another 'Jones' relative was the New Quay harbour master, an old man when introduced to Bill's own young son many years later. These appear to be the halcyon days for Bill and his sister, away from life's pressures.

John Rees with Grandson Richard

John continued his work as a mine electrician, being employed in a number of mines, as a surface worker. His additional training, no doubt gave him a range of opportunities. Bill's recollections of his father were of a technically skilled man, excellent at his job, but who did not 'suffer fools gladly'. He was not beyond walking out of a job if the situation was not to his liking. This led to a few rather lean periods for the family. Bill recalled one Christmas when the Christmas dinner was 'beans on toast'. Actually, as a youngster, beans may have been preferable to Turkey!

Started in the US, 'Heinz Beanz' were produced in South London from 1905. The earliest cans were produced before can openers were widespread so the company's literature detailed how to open the canister – by stabbing it with a knife! Its popularity grew, as a safe and convenient food, and during World War 2, Britain's Ministry of Food declared beans to be essential and exempt from rationing.

Enid Hughes (nee Rees) and daughter

Enid, married Idris Hughes at the age of 26 years. The couple had one daughter. Tragically, Enid drowned in 1960, in Porthcawl.

Enid Hughes (nee Rees)

Bill matriculated from Aberdare Boys' Grammar School and then went on to complete a five-year apprenticeship in engineering, based at the Werfa Dare Colliery, in Aberdare. This had included both mechanical and electrical engineering. A few months after completing his apprenticeship, in 1935, he joined the Royal Air Force as an aircraft engine fitter. The early years of his service were based at various locations in the south of England. Then, in 1937, he was posted to serve on the 'HMS Glorious', an aircraft carrier based at the time, in the Mediterranean. At that time, the RAF served on RN ships (aircraft carriers). Two years later, as war broke out, Bill was promoted to Corporal. He took leave, and married Edith Mary Kinnersley (known as Edie) in February the following year. As was common-place at that time, the couple had to be married by special licence due to the constraints of time.

Bill Rees and his bride Edith Kinnersley, married February 1939.

Bill returned to duty but did not re-join the 'Glorious'. The aircraft carrier was on its way to support operations in Norway. It was while evacuating British Aircraft from Norway, in June 1940, that the 'Glorious' was sunk in the North Sea, with the tragic loss of 1,200 lives. Knowing many of the men who had lost their lives must have been devastating for Bill, along with the shock of what might have been, but for his marriage.

Over the war period, Bill became expert in his work, maintaining a wide range of aircraft engines. He served for two years in the Mediterranean and was then posted to the East, where he served in Singapore, West Ceylon, China Bay and Southern India. By 1943, he had risen to the position of Flight Sergeant. Along with many young men, Bill was discharged from the RAF in 1945, at the end of the war. The war was not without incident for him, he was badly injured when an aircraft propeller hit and shattered his right arm and suffered more than one severe infection while in the East, all of which required significant periods of hospitalisation.

Bill returned home, to Edie and his young son, still living in his home town, Aberdare. He took up local engineering work and then moved on to work for the Ministry of Aviation. Their second son was born, and for a while, Bill's father John lived with them. Edie would recount that John, in his later years was a difficult man to please. As a man who had always known his own mind and had been used to his independence, it is probable that being answerable to the head of house, who was not now himself, was proving uncomfortable.

Unfortunately, the war had taken its toll. Bill had been susceptible to anxiety from a young age, but his mental health had taken a battering and he was in need of long term medical input. With changes of place of work, within the Ministry of Aviation, the family moved many times. Unfortunately, Bill's health seemed to decline. The couple's youngest son was born in the mid-1950s. Bill finally retired through ill-health in 1964. Medical input would see him in and out of hospital for a number of years and subjected to a range of quite experimental treatments, including surgery. Treatments that would today be seen as barbaric and inhumane.

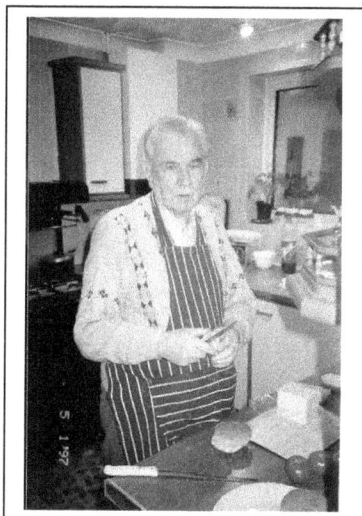

Throughout this period, Edie remained firmly by his side. Every change of house was subjected to her home-making and she took comfort in her sons and the normality that they brought to the domestic scene. The couple were finally able to live a relatively peaceful life, Bill taking solace in his woodwork and cooking. They saw all their boys married and enjoyed time spent with their grandchildren.

Theirs was another home always filled with the smell of baking, a favourite being Welsh cakes – no-one ever quite achieved the same mouth-watering recipe.

Edie had her own medical issues, that were borne bravely. She died in 1999, when her body finally succumbed to pancreatic cancer. Bill died in 2006, aged 92.

Happy Times
Dennis and Eirwen Edwards (ends) Bill and Edie Rees (centre)

The Morris Family

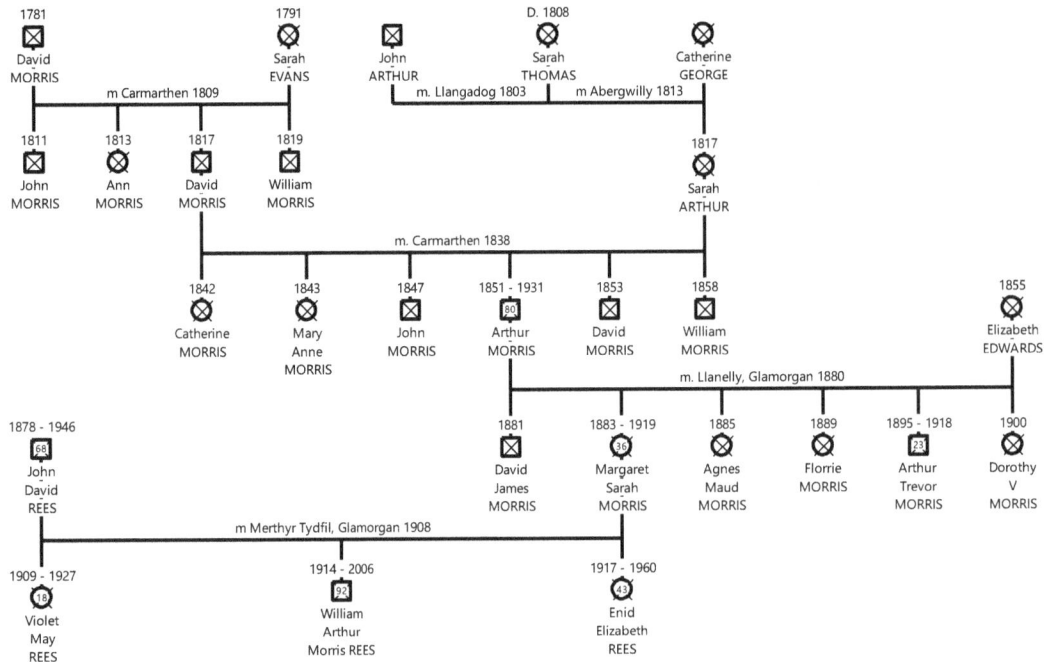

The earliest Morris ancestors came from Carmarthen. David Morris (Bill's 3xG Grandfather) was a shoe-maker, born around 1781. He married Sarah Evans and they had four children: John, who became a hatter, Ann, David, and William, who became a cooper.

Their son David started his working life as a tin man and then tin plate worker. He married Sarah, a local girl, the daughter of John Arthur, a fisherman. Sarah's mother was Catherine, John's second wife, but Sarah had been named after John's first wife, born Sarah Thomas. The couple married in St Peter's Church, Carmarthen, Sarah 'signing' with a cross. Five of their six children: Catherine, Mary Ann, John, Arthur and David, were then born in Carmarthen, before the couple moved to Gloucester Street, in Aberdare. Their youngest son, William was born there. By this time David was in his early forties, trading as a plumber.

In the 1840s and 1850s, the title 'tinman' was used for craftsmen who worked with metal to produce a wide range of products. In later centuries, they were often called 'tin smiths', 'tin plate workers' or 'sheet metal workers'. These were men who dealt in all things metal. As an apprentice, a tinsmith would have learned the art of soldering metal objects together using tinman's solder. To transfer his trade to that of plumbing or gas fitting would cause him no difficulty, he would use plumbers' solder to join lead water or gas pipes together, the jobs needed the same tools, a heat source for heating the soldering iron, the correct type of solder (tinman's or plumbers') and a tin of flux.

David and his wife Sarah set up a shop and tinworks at 17 Duke Street. This was also their home. Arthur and David both followed their father into the tin trade and they continued the shop and tinworks after their parents' deaths, both in the mid-1870s. Even after Arthur's marriage to Elizabeth Edwards and the growth of their family, David remained with them. The tin business grew and included brass work, plumbing and gas working.

Arthur and Elizabeth named their first son David James, after his late father. Then, followed Margaret Sarah (Maggie), Agnes Maud (Maud), Florence Ethel (Florrie), Arthur Trevor (Trevor) and Dorothy (Dolly). We know from the 1911 Census, that six more babies died in infancy.

109

As soon as David James was old enough, he joined the family business.

Almost certainly, the first gas work that would have been offered was gas lighting. The advantages of gas lighting had been well advertised, freedom from sparks that could cause fires, the absence of smoke and the steadiness and intensity of the flame, making it very popular. The manufacture and installation of one-and-a-half inch pipes, made of tinned iron with soldered joints would probably have taken up a great deal of their time. In 1894, Arthur applied for a patent.

> *Patent No. 8,028*
>
> *April 23rd, 1894 - A. Morris, Aberdare, Glamorganshire   Oil lamps and Match-holders*
>
> *This relates to those miners' lamps which are provided with a removable shank by which the lamp is held, and comprises the combination of a match receptacle with the lamp. A shank is made in two separate parts, one forming the match receptacle, and is screw-threaded to correspond either with a reservoir mount or with a burner mount. The shank may be made in one piece, closed at the end by a removable stopper.*
>
> *Aberdare Leader*

Arthur Morris outside his shop

Arthur took over a workshop at the site of the Aberdare Market Hall. The business was clearly expanding and the new workshop would allow for an increase in staff and more space for tools and other equipment. Life though was not without its troubles. In 1900, a 'receiving order' was declared for bad debts, with liabilities totalling £322 17s. The causes of the failure were attributed to 'Insufficient capital, bad trade, and keen competition.' It is probable that the growth in the use of electricity, particularly for lighting, was significantly limiting a formerly profitable area of their trade. This must have been a difficult period for Arthur and his family, but his tenacity and determination ensured that the business did not close. The shop and workshop were maintained.

In 1901, there were five such workshops, the Morris and Son tin workshop, a hairdresser, a cycle shop, a fish shop and a hay and corn stores. A devastating fire that occurred the following year, suggests that a further workshop existed, or perhaps one changed hands, because it was suspected that the fire started at a paint workshop. The Market Hall was saved, but the interior was gutted, fire destroying the wares of almost all traders. The total insurance cost was around £12,000.

It is difficult to know how the fire affected the Morris's, but it is unlikely they were unscathed by the event. What is clear, is that they went on trading and were technically innovative in their pursuit of new business.

In 1907, David James Morris, at the age of 26, applied for a patent. It was published later the same year. He had developed improvements to Acetylene Gas Generators:

Application Number 190707812   COMPLETE SPECIFICATION

I, DAVID JAMES MORRIS, of 17, Duke Street, Aberdare, in the County of Glamorgan, Plumber and Gasfitter, do hereby declare the nature of this invention and in what manner the same is to be performed to be particularly described and ascertained in and by the following statement:
Our invention relates to acetylene gas generators designed for use in connection with portable lamps or for street or other lighting and has for its object to provide improved means for ensuring that a portion only of the charge of calcium carbide shall be wetted at one time and that this, portion shall be practically exhausted before the water flows to the next portion of the charge and so on.

According to our invention the carbide holder or container which is advantageously of cylindrical shape and is divided into a series of compartments in a well-known manner, is provided with a perforated trough or tray which forms the lid of the container and which may be hinged or otherwise connected to the latter so that as the carbide expands during the netting it will not lift the said lid. In practice, the quantity of carbide placed in each of the several compartments should be such that when it has expanded to its fullest extent it will press closely against the underside of the said trough and practically close the perforations. This carbide holder is mounted in a cylinder or chamber into which the water, in regulated quantities, is allowed to flow from a tank or reservoir arranged above the said cylinder, the arrangement of the connection being such that when the carbide container is in position the water will drop into the said perforated trough at one end thereof.

The pipe or channel through which the water flows from the tank or reservoir to the carbide chamber is provided with a small orifice at the end within the said tank and has arranged within it a wire of polygonal cross section passing through the said orifice and preferably carried upon a screw-plug. By rotating the said plug the wire serves to dislodge any deposit from the water which may block the orifice.

Within the following few years, David obviously felt that he could have better prospects abroad and so he emigrated to the USA.

Arthur and Elizabeth's other children took different routes. Maggie married John Rees and remained at 17, Duke Street until after the birth of their first daughter Violet Mary (May). She died of influenza in 1919 aged 35 years. Florrie married and moved to Pontyclyn, near LLanelly.

At the beginning of World War 1, Trevor enlisted with the Welsh Regiment, 34th Battalion, Machine Gun Corps (Infantry). He served in Western Europe and it was in France and Flanders that he was killed in action. He died just weeks before the end of the war, in July 1918, at the age of 23 years. His name is on the memorial at Soissons. He has no known grave.

Dolly married James Llewellyn in 1922. James died of pneumoconiosis in 1954, aged 57 years. He would presumably have been suffering from ill-health for some time. Pneumoconiosis is also known as 'black lung' and is caused by the long-term exposure to coal dust. The coal dust builds up in the lungs and cannot be removed by the body; leading to inflammation, fibrosis and in the worst cases, necrosis. It was a very common condition amongst coal miners at that time. Today it continues to affect mine workers, but present-day safety legislation has significantly reduced its occurrence.

Florrie and Dolly were both widowed so they 'joined forces' and lived together, into their old age.

Arthur himself, continued the tin and plumbing business until well into his old age, setting a new shop up in Lewis Street, when the family decided to move to Aberaman. He died in 1931, aged 80 years, having lost his wife nine years earlier.

The Edwards Family

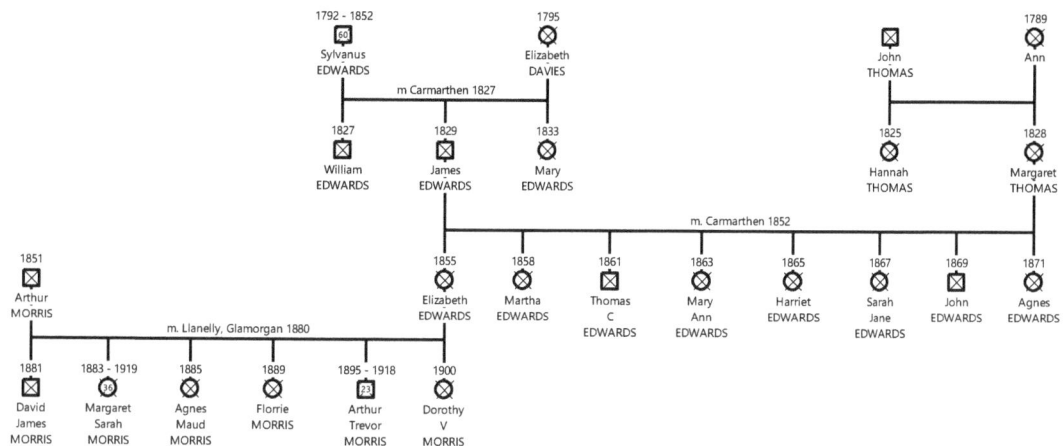

1792 - 1852 Sylvanus EDWARDS · 1795 Elizabeth DAVIES · John THOMAS · 1789 Ann

m Carmarthen 1827

1827 William EDWARDS · 1829 James EDWARDS · 1833 Mary EDWARDS · 1825 Hannah THOMAS · 1828 Margaret THOMAS

m. Carmarthen 1852

1851 Arthur MORRIS · 1855 Elizabeth EDWARDS · 1858 Martha EDWARDS · 1861 Thomas C EDWARDS · 1863 Mary Ann EDWARDS · 1865 Harriet EDWARDS · 1867 Sarah Jane EDWARDS · 1869 John EDWARDS · 1871 Agnes EDWARDS

m. Llanelly, Glamorgan 1880

1881 David James MORRIS · 1883 - 1919 Margaret Sarah MORRIS · 1885 Agnes Maud MORRIS · 1889 Florrie MORRIS · 1895 - 1918 Arthur Trevor MORRIS · 1900 Dorothy V MORRIS

The Edwards family also had roots in Carmarthen. Sylvanus Edwards, born in 1792, was a hand loom wool weaver. He and his bride, Elizabeth Davies, married at the Church of St Peter, in Carmarthen. They had three children: William, James and Mary.

James initially, took work with his father as a hand loom weaver, but following his own marriage in 1852, to Margaret Thomas, he looked for work elsewhere. The couple started married life in Carmarthen, where their first three children were born: Elizabeth, Martha and Thomas. Then, in 1861, James went to live for a while with Margaret's mother Ann, who was living in Merthyr Tydfil with her other daughter, Hannah. James had taken the opportunity, offered by his mother-in-law to stay with them while he found new work. He tried his hand as an iron worker, but, although the pay may have been better, this choice of occupation was not for him. By 1871, James and Margaret had made their home in Llanelly, Carmarthenshire. The couple had five more children: Mary Ann, Harriet, Sarah Jane, John and Agnes. They lived at Station House and James was the Station Master.

James, at around 50 years, changed job again. He became stock-taker at the tin works in Llanelly. He continued in this position for a sustained period, but at the age of 72 years, still at the tin works, took the role of check-weigher.

James and Margaret's large family gradually left the nest, towards independent lives. Eldest daughter, Elizabeth, married Arthur Morris and moved to Aberdare. Martha married David Davies, a carpenter. Their eldest son, Thomas, became a weigher, at the iron works. Mary Ann and Sarah Jane became school teachers and Harriet, a dressmaker. Agnes married William Howells, a tin plate worker. John found work as a steel furnace worker and moved in with Agnes and William after the deaths of their parents.

Afterword

So that, for the time being, is as far as we've got. There are many more records to peruse, places to visit and people to meet.

I didn't realise when we started to look, how engaging the lives of our ancestors would be. Some wealthy, some desperately poor, many courageous, selfless or deeply religious. We've been to their homes and trodden the same paths, removed ivy from their grave stones and read about them in old newspapers. We've learned of happy times and sad, of long lives and others far too short.

They now feel like part of us - they always have been, of course.

.... to be continued!